Sunnyside

Born almost at the same time that the United States was born, and named for the hero of the Revolution who became The Father of His Country, Washington Irving was a young New York dandy who became a cosmopolitan bachelor.

He was an almost English country gentleman who rode and camped out with troopers and trappers in the Far West. He was a romantic idler in castles in Spain and a hard-working diplomat in London and Madrid. He was the intimate of royal families in Europe and of Rip Van Winkle in the Catskills and of Ichabod Crane and Brom Bones in Sleepy Hollow.

Washington Irving called the home he built on the Hudson River just below Tarrytown "Sunnyside," but the name means more than that in connection with Washington Irving. It was the sunny side of life he sought and found. It was the sunny side of life he presented in his sketches, legends, stories, histories, and biographies.

What his life was actually like and what he was like you will find in the pages of *Sunnyside*.

James Playsted Wood

Sunnyside

A LIFE OF WASHINGTON IRVING

Illustrations by Antony Saris

Pantheon Books

First Printing

 Published in New York by Pantheon Books, a division of Random House, Inc., and simultaneously in Toronto, Canada, by Random House of Canada Limited.

Library of Congress Catalog Card Number: 67–20224

Manufactured in the United States of America

for Sterling Wesley Fisher

"Since then I have often remembered that sunny morning and that open window,—so suggestive of his sunny temperament and his open heart . . ."

Henry Wadsworth Longfellow,
recalling his first meeting
with Washington Irving in
Madrid in 1827.

Sunnyside

chapter I

When, November 2, 1783, George Washington made his triumphal re-entry into New York which had been occupied by the British for almost the entire period of the American Revolution, Washington Irving was already in residence. He lived at 131 William Street between John and Fulton Streets. He had been there for seven months. The child who had been named for the victorious Commander-in-Chief of the Continental Army was exactly seven months old.

Washington had been forced to withdraw his troops from the city which he knew he could not defend after the Battle of Long Island in August 1776. Some of his generals wanted to burn it to prevent its falling into British hands, but Congress demurred. The colonial forces fled north up Manhattan Island to Harlem and Washington Heights. They took a stand at the Battle of Harlem Heights—actually Morningside Heights, just above where Columbia University now stands—where General Israel Putnam with 1,800 men repulsed a smaller attacking force. In October 1776 the British commander, General William Howe, swept up the East River and drove Washington and the main body of his troops off Manhattan, back to the mainland. Some 2,000 Americans were captured when the British took Fort Washington at 183rd Street.

The British then seized the undefended city, a quarter of which was soon afterward destroyed by fire. A second and larger fire two years later devastated more of hapless New York.

The British destroyed the wealth of the city. They plundered homes, ruined businesses. They crowded thousands of prisoners into the City Hall, into the big sugar house of the Livingstons, and into King's College. Stripped of its pews, the Dutch church at Nassau and Cedar Streets was a jammed dungeon. So many ragged, half-starved prisoners slept on the floor that when one turned all had to turn. Thousands more were thrust into the dark, stinking holds of prison ships anchored in New York harbor.

One William Irving of New York was Scottish by birth. He had come from Orkney and had served as an officer aboard a British packet. Married to Sarah Sanders (born in England the grand-daughter of a Church of England clergyman), he had settled in New York about 1763. There he had become a prosperous merchant dealing, both wholesale and retail, as was then the custom, in general merchandise, but particularly in hardware and wines.

Because of his marked and unswerving sympathy with the cause of independence, William Irving and his family suffered during the Revolution. They were finally forced to flee the city for a home in Rahway, New Jersey. Even there they were singled out. When the British invaded New Jersey, they commandeered the best rooms in the Irving home. The large family had to make out as best it could in the attic. A stern, strictly religious man, Irving was undeterred. He persisted in his patriotism and in helping Americans who were worse off than he.

The prison hulks in the harbor—the *Jersey* in Wallabout Bay was perhaps the worst—were infamous. The cruelty of the guards was the only diversion from starvation and disease. Every night the prisoners were locked into the holds. In the morning the guards called through the iron gratings, "Rebels, turn out your dead!" Only the hardiest survived. Some 11,000 bodies are said to have been ferried to the Brooklyn shore for burial in shallow graves. For a long time the tides washed up human bones.

William Irving did what he could for the prisoners who managed to stay alive. At the end of the bitter war a Presbyterian minister certified: "Deacon William Irving, merchant in this city . . . contributed largely to my relief and was probably an instrument under God in the preservation of my life—and by credible accounts I have had from other prisoners, both in this city and in the country, has been the means of the preservation of theirs also."

The acts which endeared William Irving to his fellows did not endear him to the British. The family was forced to remain in Rahway two years. It was shortly after their return to New York that, April 3, 1783, Washington Irving was born. He was the youngest of eleven children. Three had died in infancy, but he had four brothers and three sisters. His oldest brother, William, was nearly seventeen.

For the first five months of his life, Washington Irving was legally a British subject. The Treaty of Paris, which ended the war and established the independence of the thirteen states of the United States, was not signed until September 3, 1783. The British military evacuated New York that month.

General Henry Knox and his men moved down Bowery Lane from Harlem. November 2, they joined General Washington at the Bull's Head Tavern. From there Washington and his staff, together with the New York governor and his suite, marched downtown eight abreast. The retreating English had left their Union Jack flying atop Fort George at the Battery on the southern tip of Manhattan Island. An American sailor who had to nail cleats across the pole for footholds as he mounted, threw down the British ensign, and ran up the American flag.

Congress demobilized the Continental Army. At Fraunces Tavern on December 4 (the West Indian, Samuel Fraunces, became the first President's steward) George Washington bade farewell to his officers. He resigned his commission that month, and two days before Christmas retired to Mount Vernon.

"Washington's work is done," Irving's mother is supposed to have said, "and the child shall be named after him." She chose the name well, but she was wrong about George Washington.

Washington Irving's birth, boyhood, and youth were thus coeval with the birth and early years of the republic of the United States. This was a circumstance which was to prove fortunate for both the man and the country.

The small, war-damaged, fire-devastated city at the southern end of Manhattan began to rebuild hurriedly as soon as the Revolutionary War was over, and it recovered quickly. It was back to business for the city and its merchants. The Irving family business got under way again, and it thrived.

The great New York harbor soon filled with ships as the city reasserted its commercial life. Often there were one hundred at anchor or at dockside. New York was the chief trading center of the new country, and very soon it became its capital. In 1784 Congress elected to meet in New York and the next year went into session in Federal Hall on Wall Street. King's College, which had been a prison, then a hospital, became Columbia College. DeWitt Clinton, a nephew of the governor of New York, was on his way to enroll in the College of New Jersey at Princeton when he stopped en route and became instead the first student in Columbia.

The Constitution of the United States was drawn up in Philadelphia in 1787. Backed by Alexander Hamilton and James Madison, it was strongly favored in Federalist New York. New York adopted it in a state convention held in Poughkeepsie, about seventy-five miles up the Hudson from New York City, and New York held a giant celebration.

There was a great parade July 23, 1788. All the trades and professions marched to the music of military bands. Columbia students, ministers, bankers, carpenters, and all the rest took part in a procession that was a mile and a half long and kept going from eight o'clock in the morning until five in the afternoon. There were elaborate floats with coopers making barrels on one and bakers baking bread on another. The bakers made a huge loaf which they called the Federal Loaf and marked it into thirteen slices for the thirteen states.

The biggest float of all was the Federal ship *Hamilton*. Drawn by ten horses, it was a ship under full sail, a thirty-two-gun frigate manned by thirty seamen and marines. Every now and again as it sailed down Broadway the *Hamilton* stopped to give a thirteen-gun salute. George Washington watched it all from the reviewing stand at Fort George on the Battery.

Washington Irving watched it too. He could hardly have missed the great parade. New York was one glorious celebration, with the staid Noah Webster, the Chamber of Commerce, and visiting gentlemen marching along with laborers and veterans of the Revolution. Though the five-year-old boy may have understood little of what it was all about, he must have been caught up in the sound and color.

This was only the beginning of the excitement. Major Pierre Charles L'Enfant remodeled the City Hall on Wall Street—even then the most important business street in the country—as a capitol for the United States. Preparations got under way for the inauguration of George Washington as President. Samuel Osgood's house at 3 Cherry Street was got ready as the presidential palace.

In April 1789, George Washington embarked at Elizabethtown Point, New Jersey, in a specially built forty-five-foot barge manned by thirteen harbor pilots in white uniforms. The barge landed at the Battery to a thirteen-gun salute and the cheering of the crowds. Washington (who had had to borrow £600 for his expenses) stepped out and mounted the carpeted stairs. He wore his customary buff-and-blue uniform.

Inauguration Day was April 30. There were church services in the morning. The procession which had formed to wait on George Washington at Cherry Street moved with solemn dignity to Wall Street where a striped awning had been hung over the balcony of Federal Hall. Chancellor Robert Livingston administered the oath of office to George Washington, who for this solemn occasion was dressed in brown homespun and wore his dress sword. Washington kissed the Bible. Livingston waved his hat to the crowds. The swelling cheer went up. "Long live George Washington, President of the United States!"

These were great events. These were memorable scenes. New York was an exciting place for an impressionable child to grow up in.

Cannon roared. Bells pealed. The crowds shouted their ecstasy. They cheered their heroes and the birth of the nation. That night there were fireworks at the Battery. So great was the throng that Washington, who watched the display from the Livingston house at 3 Broadway, had to walk home. His carriage could not get through the milling crowds.

The riotous celebration went on for a week. Members of the new government in which Alexander Hamilton was Secretary of the Treasury; Samuel Osgood, Postmaster General; John Jay, Chief Justice of the Supreme Court, were all there. Foreign diplomats accredited to the brand new—and some of them thought ridiculous—

country were there. The Irving family were there with all the rest of Manhattan's populace, and its youngest member met the President once, perhaps twice.

"I remember George Washington perfectly. There was some occasion when he appeared in a public procession; my nurse, a good old Scotch woman, was very anxious for me to see him, and held me up in her arms as he rode past. This, however, did not satisfy her; so the next day when walking with me in Broadway, she espied him in a shop, she seized my hand, and darting in, exclaimed in her bland Scotch, 'Please, your excellency, here's a bairn that's called after ye!' General Washington then turned his benevolent face full upon me, smiled, laid his hand upon my head, and gave me his blessing, which . . . I have reason to believe has attended me through life. I was but five years old, yet I can feel that hand upon my head even now."

Washington Irving told that story happily many times during his life. Sometimes he told it a little differently. As, many years later, he recounted it to the boy George Havens Putnam, son of his American publisher, there had been more to the first meeting with his lifelong hero than the usual story showed. "My nurse told me afterwards that the General lifted me up in his arms to the pommel of his saddle and bestowed upon me a formal blessing."

Whether the Father of his country blessed the creator of Rip Van Winkle and the first internationally celebrated American writer once or twice, the results seem to have been as happy as Washington Irving always believed.

New York, 1789. Federal Hall

chapter II

Before Washington Irving was a year old the family moved across the street into 128 William. If the description by his nephew, Pierre Munro Irving, is correct, it was an odd house. On a lot with only a 25-foot frontage but more than 150 feet deep, it was really two houses, one in front, one in back, joined by a central building. The roofs were at different heights, and there were plenty of odd angles. It was an ideal place for climbing, but the smallest of the young Irvings did not climb the roofs or the apricot and plum trees in the garden when his father was about.

William Irving was as strict at home as he was prosperous in business. There were family prayers every day, and attendance was compulsory. William Irving looked upon work as virtuous but on play as sinful, and he was against it. The children had one half-holiday a week from school. He saw to it that they spent this undue leisure in study of the Westminster Catechism of the Presbyterian Church. The Presbyterians in New York were worshipping in the Episcopal Chapel of St. George while they built a new church when Washington Irving was christened. Thus he began life in one persuasion under the hospitable roof of another. Sundays meant church in the morning and in the afternoon and a religious lecture at night. In between—if they could stay awake, and often Washington could not—they were allowed to read *Pilgrim's Progress.*

Church was so much more familiar to them than any other scene or activity outside the home that playing at preaching and taking the sacrament was a favorite pastime with the younger Irving children.

When he was four years old, Washington Irving began to attend a school kept by a Mrs. Ann Kilmaster on Ann Street between William and Gold Streets. There he learned the alphabet. Two years later he was entered in a school for both boys and girls kept by Benjamin Romaine at 198 Fulton Street. Small for his years, handsome and precocious, Washington Irving was a favorite with the master as he was a favorite with his brothers and sisters at home. For obvious reasons, Romaine, a veteran of the Revolution, called his pupil "General."

Irving, who was to have a lifelong passion for the theater, made his theatrical debut at the Romaine school. He may not have played his part too well, but he convulsed the audience. The play was Joseph Addison's *Cato*, and Washington Irving, aged eleven, played the part of Juba, Prince of Numidia. When the cue came for him to go on, the small prince was offstage eating sticky honey cake. He had no time either to swallow it or get rid of it. When he found himself before the footlights and the audience, he could not speak. The reason was simple. His mouth was gummed up with cake. He had to hook it out with a forefinger before he could get out his lines. The audience was delighted.

Affectionate and romantically inclined from his early years, Washington Irving was usually in love with someone. At this time it was with a girl in the cast of the play who was a head taller than he. Charitably she told him that he was handsome and that she liked him but that he was too little. "I renounced my tall mistress and went back to my honey cake," Irving said.

Irving was a passable but not an industrious scholar. He had the bright world of New York all around him and the even brighter world he found at home in the books of a family with literary tastes. School could not compete with these stronger attractions.

During the year that New York was the capital of the United States, George Washington drove about in his canary-colored coach drawn by six white horses with painted hoofs. Other men and women of fashion took the air in their coaches and carriages. A favorite drive was up Third Avenue and along the Boston Post Road, across Murray Hill, and back down the Hudson through Greenwich Village, an excursion of about fourteen miles. Murray Hill and Greenwich were then outlying villages. New

York itself did not extend above Chambers Street, now merely the northern boundary of the financial district of lower Manhattan. Above Chambers Street was the open country.

People in this city of less than 60,000 were so certain that New York was unlikely to extend farther that the front of a new City Hall was faced with marble but the back, facing Chambers Street, only with brownstone. Few people, thought the architects, were apt to see it.

Wall Street was the center of business and government, but the end toward Broadway opposite tall Trinity Church was a fashionable residential section. Many leading New York families, including the Hamiltons, lived there. Baker's Hotel was there. The famed Tontine Coffee House, where merchants and brokers gathered, was at the corner of Wall and Water Streets. The theater was on John Street. All of this was only a few blocks from where the Irvings lived on William. George Washington went occasionally to the John Street Theater, and once at a performance of a comedy titled *Darby's Return* the unsmiling great man was seen to laugh. People were awed.

New York was gay and prosperous. In winter there were skating and sleighing parties. There was always a great celebration on New Year's Day. In summer there were picnics in the country. The capital was moved to Philadelphia, and the dignitaries of government left New York. People were sorry to see them leave, but not disconsolate. From the beginning New York was a market place and a money mart. Its aristocrats were men of business and property. The gayety and prosperity went on.

Going to and from school, Washington Irving could

smell the sea and see the masts of the tall ships docked in the East and the North River or watch them swaying at anchor off the Battery. The promenade across the wide lawns and under the tall trees where the ocean slapped against the sea walls was where George Washington liked to walk for his daily exercise. The Battery was a favorite haunt of his namesake too. On the way home he eyed the John Street Theater wistfully.

Some of the ships he saw brought the merchandise from abroad which his father and the other merchants sold. Irving dreamed of the places from which and to which they sailed. He knew something of the sea and foreign lands. A favorite book was *Robinson Crusoe*. Another was *Robin Hood*. He read *Orlando Furioso*, Ariosto's long poem of knights and ladies in the time of Charlemagne.

His older brothers belonged to literary societies and mingled in the literary as well as the fashionable mercantile world of New York. He listened to their talk and began early to share their tastes. His own at this time was principally for the delights he found in twenty small volumes of travel in the family library. He read and re-read these volumes of *The World Displayed*. He was so fascinated by what he read of Spain and the Orient that he decided to run away to sea.

To prepare himself for the hardships of life before the mast, the small boy forced himself to eat salt pork, which he detested. He slept on the floor, which was the only deck he had at hand. The salt pork was too distasteful, and the floor was too hard. Irving, who had a catlike love of comfort—though he could face down discomfort and even hardship when he had to—gave up the idea.

In 1793, when Irving was ten years old, his oldest brother, William, married Julia Paulding of Tarrytown, a Westchester village about twenty-five miles up the wide Hudson from New York. Irving, whose early and middle life was so deeply influenced by his brothers, gained through this event. It brought him the lifelong friendship of the bride's brother, James Kirke Paulding.

Irving already knew the woods and fields of upper Manhattan and the banks of the Hudson. Through Paulding he came to know the country farther north and those parts of beautiful Westchester County which he made Irving country in his legends and stories. Irving and Paulding roamed the woods and fields together, sometimes in search of squirrels and other small game. It was also Paulding, four years older than Irving, who introduced him to a forbidden and longed-for delight. When visiting his sister and her husband, Paulding took Irving with him to the John Street Theater to see Joseph Jefferson act in *Speculation.*

His father disapproved of the theater which he considered wicked. Irving considered it wonderful, and it was readily accessible. After family prayers at night, he would slip out the back to see as much of every play as he could, slip back in after the performance, and appear innocently from his room in the morning.

After ten years in Romaine's school, Irving went for a time to a school kept by Josiah A. Henderson on John Street. Here he studied Latin, the only classical education he ever received. He took music lessons. He studied drawing at which he proved adept, and secretly he took dancing lessons. His father disapproved of dancing. Also in secret,

Irving had himself confirmed in the Episcopal Church, though obediently he continued to attend his father's Presbyterian Church.

His older brothers, Peter and John, had attended Columbia. For some reason, Washington Irving was not sent there after them. It is unlikely he argued the point. Columbia would have meant study, and Irving preferred pleasure.

Like their father, William Irving was a successful young businessman. Peter had wished to study law, but their father disapproved. He did not consider the law an honest profession. Peter had then studied medicine. He became Dr. Peter Irving, though he never practiced. John Treat Irving first studied for the ministry. When he found this not to his liking he, too, asked to study law. This time the father relented and, in time, this son became Judge John Irving. This set a precedent which Washington Irving was allowed to follow. At sixteen he began his apprenticeship in the law office of Henry Brockholst Livingston.

When his mentor was appointed a judge of the New York Supreme Court, Irving transferred to the law office of Josiah Ogden Hoffman. Hoffman and his family were to be of far greater importance to the imaginative and pleasure-loving Washington Irving than the law would ever be. To his legal studies he paid what was sometimes very little attention but more often no attention at all.

Of far greater interest to him were his travels which began at this time and continued over far greater distances and much longer periods for the greater part of his life.

The urge to go and see and hear and taste and ponder

what he experienced was strong in Washington Irving. He liked to wander, to stroll, to observe. The new, the distant, and the picturesque drew him always. He was the curious and reflective observer by nature. If there were a place to go, Washington Irving wanted to go there, and usually he went.

There were no railroads. There were not even steamboats yet. A journey of one hundred miles took more planning and preparation than a trip around the world might take today. The traveler moved slowly in a sailboat or on a river barge. He rode on a horse or in a carriage, a stagecoach, a chaise, or a wagon. Once out of the city or the town, the roads were bad, barely passable or nonexistent.

The distances between towns and cities were long. Even in the east there were few large centers. Most of the time the traveler was in lonely country or in wilderness with the frontier not too far away.

To the imaginative Irving the anticipation of a journey was a delight in itself and the actual excursion a happy realization. He liked comfort, but he could support hardship if it brought him the rewards of motion, new scenes, strange faces, quaint inns, and country characters.

As usual, it was his affectionate brothers and sisters who led the way and made realization of his wishes possible. Irving had spent holidays in Westchester in 1798 and wandered, gun in hand, through the Sleepy Hollow country near Tarrytown. He made his first voyage the navigable length of the Hudson when he went to visit his oldest sister, Ann.

Ann had married Richard Dodge, a surveyor on the

Mohawk River. Dodge had persuaded William Irving to join him in setting up a post on the frontier, then only about forty miles west of Albany. The two young men did well trading in furs with the Indians. William stayed at the post four years, then returned to New York, where he went into business for himself as a merchant, setting up shop at 208 Broadway. Dodge and Ann then moved to Johnstown, New York.

Irving's second sister, Catherine, had met and married a young lawyer named Daniel Paris who had attended Columbia with Peter Irving. She, too, lived in Johnstown. It was to visit his sisters that Washington Irving made his first journey into upper New York to the settlement of Johnstown, about forty-eight miles west of Albany. It was strange, exciting, different. The visit gave Washington Irving his first experience of the wilderness world.

Irving made a second visit to Johnstown in 1802, but this time he was not as happy there. He wrote a friend in the city, "I have been unwell almost all the time I have been up here. I am too weak to take any exercise, and too low-spirited half the time to enjoy company. My chief amusements are reading, drawing, and writing letters —the two latter I have to do more sparingly than I could wish, on account of the pain in my breast."

The pain alarmed him and alarmed his family. At that time, tuberculosis was the dread and often fatal disease. With good reason, any symptom of pulmonary illness frightened people. The depression he felt was as characteristic of Washington Irving as the elation he often felt and showed. All through life his moods changed quickly. He was often merry, entertaining, the best of company.

Almost as often he was dispirited. He was always easily hurt, easily discouraged.

Both illness and depression seemed to vanish when he returned to New York. Oliver Goldsmith was one of the favorite authors of James Paulding, and Irving shared his liking for the popular author of the *Vicar of Wakefield*, *She Stoops to Conquer*, and *The Deserted Village*. Like everyone else at the time who read at all, he knew the witty and whimsical essays of Joseph Addison and Richard Steele. In the manner of these writers, the eighteen-year-old Washington Irving wrote a series of satirical letters. They described lightly and humorously New York social and theatrical life.

Irving had no trouble finding a market for his wares. As his older brothers had stimulated and guided his literary tastes, one of them became his first publisher. Dr. Peter Irving was at this time the editor of a newspaper, the *Morning Chronicle*, as well as of another paper, the *Corrector*, which supported Aaron Burr.

Peter ran the amusing letters by "Jonathan Oldstyle, Gent." in the *Chronicle*. People read them, liked them, and praised them. Vice President Aaron Burr clipped them out and sent them to his daughter, Theodosia, whom he was bringing up to be a young woman of intellect as well as fashion. The letters were very good for so young an author, he told her. They drew favorable comment from others and even attracted the attention of Charles Brockden Brown, Philadelphia novelist, who called on the flattered young author and asked him to write for his *Literary Magazine and American Register*. Still making dutiful pretense of studying law, Irving did not accept.

Washington Irving was already a published author when in the summer of 1803 he made a much longer journey. Josiah Ogden Hoffman, with whom he read law, was a leader of the New York bar and a leader of the Federalist party. He had been attorney-general of New York and had a lucrative state-wide practice. Eloquent in the courtroom, he was a man of fashion, of many aristocratic connections, and of many interests. One of these was the development of towns on his large real estate holdings. It was in pursuit of this that Hoffman and his family, Irving with them, traveled.

Hoffman's first wife had died. The year before he had married again. Irving said that Maria Fenno Hoffman was like a sister to him, and he was the intimate of all the family which, at this time, consisted of Hoffman's four children, one of them a small girl named Matilda.

Irving, now twenty, was the gay companion on this long trip through upper New York and into Canada. Though he was short, but five feet seven inches, he was handsome. His features were refined. His large, dark eyes were expressive. That his health was delicate only added to the appeal of the gifted youth whose disposition was happy and whose manners were gallant. Women liked Irving, and Irving delighted always in attractive feminine companionship. He wanted to be liked, and he was used to being liked.

It was a pleasant long summer excursion for all the Hoffman party, but sometimes when the wheels of their carriages jolted over rutted or rocky roads or when storms came up or when leaky boats tossed them about on riverways it was far more arduous than they had expected.

At one point a party of Indians took Irving into their tribe in solemn ceremony. Dancing and chanting about him, the Indians gave him the name of "Vomonte," meaning "good to everybody." Irving shrank from the exhibition. Like many humorists, he could never bear the slightest suspicion of being made the butt of a joke. He feared he looked ridiculous to the others. He felt easier when, somewhat maliciously, he connived at having Hoffman honored in a similar ceremony.

Not only was travel often difficult, but also some of the inns at which they stopped were unsavory. One inn kept by a squat French woman was so dirty that Irving relieved his distaste by writing in pencil over the fireplace:

> Here Sovereign Dirt erects her sable throne,
> The House, the host, the hostess, all her own.

The society and circumstances in Montreal, Irving found far more to his liking. Judge Hoffman was a wealthy and important figure. The partners of the powerful North West Company, which had a monopoly of the lucrative fur trade in Canada, wined and dined the visitors, and the youthful Irving responded happily to the lavish hospitality. He liked to be well served and well fed. He liked polite society, and he also liked the romance of wilderness life he heard described in the talk of the North West men.

It was on this occasion in Montreal that Irving met the man who would become his close companion in New York, his intimate friend, one who was to aid him often and in many ways.

The Brevoorts were one of the wealthiest and most influential of the old New York families. They had come to the city early in the seventeenth century and were large landowners there. Besides their property in the city, they held extensive tracts in the country outside. Henry Brevoort, Sr. had a mansion way out at Fifth Avenue and Ninth Street. People drove from the city to see the bear and the two deer which he kept in his garden, where he set traps for the quail that graced his table.

John Jacob Astor had been considered fortunate when he married a cousin of the young Henry Brevoort whom Washington Irving met in Montreal. This Henry Brevoort was then working for the Astor fur interests. Said to have been the first white man to see the straits of Mackinack, Brevoort traveled the wilderness to trade with Indians and trappers. He brought the pelts back to Albany by packhorse and canoe for shipping down the Hudson to New York.

Brevoort had a dual appeal for Irving. He was of the socially and financially elite of New York from whom the young Irvings chose their friends. He was also a businessman who dealt in the romance of the savage wilderness as well as in money. Irving would never be a successful man of business, but he would be an adventurer for most of his life.

He returned to New York stimulated by travel but not greatly improved in health. Listlessly, he went back to the study of law. Always concerned for him, his brothers watched anxiously, and they reached a decision. What he needed was a change of scene and occupation. A long sea voyage, sight of places and people he had dreamed of when he poured over *The World Displayed*, might improve Washington's health and enable him to develop the literary talents of which they felt assured.

William, Peter, Ebenezer, and John, all of them prospering then, decided to send their brother abroad. As the scions of well-to-do English families had done for generations, this youngest son of a mercantile New York family would make his grand tour of Europe.

On May 19, 1804, Washington Irving boarded ship in New York for Bordeaux in France. The sailing-ship's captain who watched his frail passenger come aboard reflected that this was a chap who would be overboard before they got across. He was wrong. Health and high spirits returned to Irving on the long voyage. When Irving had a horse or wheels under him or billowing sails were thrusting him into the golden unknown, Irving was all elation. He moved toward the lands of which he had dreamed with eagerness and determination. He had escaped the dullness of the law. He had proved that he could write. He would see and hear and record. He would enjoy all that he could enjoy and put up with all the rest. Soon after landing he wrote William:

> There is nothing I dread more than to be taken for one of the Smellfungi of this world. I therefore endeavor to be pleased with everything about me, and with the masters, mistresses, and servants of the inns, particularly when I perceive they have "all the dispositions in the world" to serve me . . .

There is much of Irving in this. He wished to be known not as one of the vulgar but as a pleasant and gentlemanly young traveler. He classed himself with the ladies and gentlemen of the world, not with his social inferiors. He had been favored and protected at home. There were always servants on William Street. Irving expected to be well served.

He was also possessed of a certain hardihood. Courage as well as fastidiousness is part of a gentleman's privilege. He hoped for the serene and pleasant. If he had to, he could endure the less pleasant with at least outward equanimity. This was an attitude and practice which Washington Irving never abandoned, and it served him well.

chapter III

Invigorated by the salt air, the freedom, the prospect of delights in store, Irving was clambering the rigging of the ship before they had been long at sea. He was like a boy let out of school, which in a way was what he was. He was twenty-one and happy.

Forty-two days after leaving New York, they made port at Bordeaux. All Europe, and especially France, was in ferment. The Corsican, Napoleon Bonaparte, was just about to declare himself emperor of France and to make himself emperor of as much of the world as he could conquer. All Europe was astir, and young Irving found it an exciting place.

He went from Bordeaux to Paris, then to Marseilles, thence to Genoa where he learned that Aaron Burr had killed Alexander Hamilton in their duel at Weehawken, across the Hudson from New York in New Jersey. He traveled through scenic Italy by stagecoach. On the way to Sicily his ship was captured by pirates. Off Medina he saw Admiral Nelson's fleet on Mediterranean patrol. The countryside, the sculpture and paintings, the antiquities, the people everywhere gripped his imagination more than the stirring events of the time.

In Rome he met the painter, only a few years older than he, who bore the same given name, Washington Allston. They became close and lasting friends. Allston taught Irving to appreciate painting, and Irving became so enthused that for a time he considered giving up his literary ambitions to become an artist. Though he had talent and was accustomed to decorating his diaries and notebooks with graphic sketches, the desire fell away. It was really Allston's society he enjoyed. He stayed on in Rome through Holy Week to watch the colorful pageantry, but he was beginning to tire of sightseeing. He wrote Peter, "On arriving at Naples I became acquainted with an American gentleman of talents, who has made the tour of Italy. I was much diverted with the manner in which he addressed his valet de place one morning as we were going out in search of curiosities. 'Now, my friend,' said he, 'recollect, I am tired of churches, convents, palaces, galleries of paintings, subterranean passages, and great men—if you have anything else to show me, *allons!*' "

Irving, too, was getting bored with the standard show-places and show pieces. Finding and traveling with congenial companions, playing his flute, keeping on the move were more to his taste. Much to his brothers' displeasure, he rushed through the rest of Italy in order to hurry back to France in entertaining company. At one point he was arrested as a spy, but instead of being hanged was soon released and made quickly for Paris.

He planned to study in Paris. He wrote William earnestly, ". . . there is no place in Europe where a young man who wishes to improve himself, and is determined to act with prudence, can spend a certain space of time to more advantage than at Paris." He enrolled for a series of lectures in botany, chemistry, and other sciences. He even attended some of the lectures and dutifully took notes, but, despite his good intentions, he could not apply himself seriously to studies which could not compete with the other attractions of the city. Society and the theater felled the sciences. He explained, confessed, and excused himself to Peter.

> Of all the places I have seen in Europe Paris is the most fascinating, and I am well satisfied that for pleasure and amusements it must leave London far behind. . . . You will excuse the shortness and hastiness of this letter, for which I can only plead as an excuse that I am a *young man* and in *Paris.*

In his diary Irving wrote, "Had a levee of tailors, shirtmakers, bootmakers &c, to rig me out à la mode de Paris." When he left Paris and reached London in a light-gray coat, an embroidered white vest, and colored smallclothes, he quickly called in a tailor to outfit him completely anew in all his dress, "that article so important to be attended to in England."

For another three months he had another good time in his new clothes.

He was ecstatic about Mrs. Sarah Siddons, most famous actress of the day, and her performance. He saw her brother, the tragedian Charles Philip Kemble, play and actually met him at dinner in the home of a Covent Garden actress whom Kemble later married. In company with a young New Yorker, Irving made a quick tour of Oxford and Bath. Soon afterward he wrote Peter, "Curiosity cannot be kept always on the stretch," and started gladly for home. He reached New York again March 24, 1806.

After two years away from it he liked the study of law even less, but he took up disinterestedly where he had left off. Finally, though his good-humored sponsors resignedly admitted that he knew little about it, Irving was admitted to the bar in 1808.

Irving enthusiastically ignored or neglected courtrooms, wills and estates, searching titles, and everything else connected with the practice of law. Exuberantly he plunged into extra-curricular activities that were more to his taste.

Greek mythology had its Nine Muses who presided over the arts and sciences. New York of the first decade of the nineteenth century had its "Nine Worthies," and Washington Irving became one of the worthiest. He was one of the gayest of the gay "Lads of Kilkenny," who were these same Nine Worthies.

They were New York's literary sporting set, the laughing, winebibbing, gentlemanly carousers who toasted the New York belles and literature and themselves and their ambitions and everything else in sight as often and as deeply as they could.

Henry Brevoort was one of them. Though he was forty and one of the leaders in foreign trade along the East River, Willam Irving was another. James K. Paulding, Peter Irving, Ebenezer Irving, Henry Ogden, Richard McCall, David Porter, and Gouverneur Kemble were among the others. They couldn't count very well, for there were more than nine. It was a point of honor with them not to be able to count after one of their convivial dinners at Dyde's Tavern, a pub on Park Row. Here they entertained themselves and friends of their own ilk from more literary Philadelphia. When they were a little low on funds, they did themselves as well as they could at a porterhouse on the corner of John and Nassau Streets.

Then Kemble turned over to the Lads a family mansion on the Passaic River between Newark and Bellville, New Jersey. Mount Pleasant, which they quickly renamed "Cockloft Hall," was a wondrous place for eating, drinking, playing leapfrog on the lawns, and falling asleep in corners when they had worn themselves out.

In a happy phrase which Edward Woodberry used in 1903, New York literary society of the time was from the beginning "bibulous and carniverous." The Sketch Club sketched a little, talked more, and held glorious picnics in the Hoboken countryside across the Hudson. When James Fenimore Cooper founded The Bread and Cheese Club, a vote of "bread" admitted a candidate to membership, but one of "cheese" told him to "cheese it."

Henry Ogden, one of the Nine Worthies, was fumbling his way home from a literary party one night when he fell through a grating into a cellar. He said he found it a little lonely at first, but one after another his partying companions fell in too, and they spent, he said, quite a pleasant night of it. Irving loved it all. When Kemble was away visiting, he wrote him exultantly, "If those chaps in Philadelphia don't treat you better, cut and run; and, foregad, we'll hear the cocks crow in New York for three mornings at least."

Most of the Lads were burning with literary ambitions. Three of them did something about it. James Kirke Paulding, William Irving, and Washington Irving began to write a series of pamphlets. Modeled after the *Spectator* papers and their scores of imitators, they were not unusual in form, but they were unique in title and distinctive in content.

The purpose of *Salmagundi; or, the Whim-Whams and Opinions of Launcelot Langstaff, Esq., and Others* was serious. As stated in its first published number, January 24, 1807, it was simply "to instruct the young, reform the old, correct the town, and castigate the age." Because they were sure they would deserve it, the anonymous authors invited the praise of all critics in advance. "Like all true editors," they said, "we consider ourselves infallible."

Launcelot and his fellows were gentlemen and aristocrats, used to taking their pinch of snuff delicately and to looking elegantly down their noses. They believed in the best books, the best plays, the best clothes, the best food and drink, and the best society—theirs. In the twenty numbers of *Salmagundi*, which appeared periodically for just a year, they talked of anything and everything. You could put almost anything you wished into salmagundi, which was a salad of chopped meats, oil, and greens, and they did.

They mocked the celebrities of the day. They lambasted the stupidity of the mob and the stupidity and effrontery of Thomas Jefferson. They detested his democracy. They even detested his red plush breeches. They twitted the "Sophie Sparkles," who were the belles, and the "Ding Dongs," who were the beaux, of New York. They retailed the deviltries at Cockloft Hall which they peopled with eccentric characters. Christopher Cockloft was the head of the family. There was a son, Jeremy, and there were two Miss Cocklofts. There were old Negro retainers. One of them, Caesar, was a privileged family member. Even the footman had his whim-whams.

From garret to cellar the house was filled with the accumulated rubbish of the past. None of them would let go anything that bore the stamp of antiquity. The Squire himself had a profound contempt for all Frenchmen and Democrats and would have none of them about his mansion. Ghosts and visitations were welcomed.

The reason the family had only one son and two daughters was explained to delighted New York, March 20, 1807. Some of the old Squire's whim-whams verged on the really unusual. "He had got from some quack philosopher or other a notion that there was a complete analogy between children and plants, and that they ought to be both reared alike. Accordingly, he sprinkled them every morning with water, laid them out in the sun, as he did his geraniums; and if the season was remarkably dry, repeated this wise experiment three or four times of a morning. The consequence was the poor little souls died one after the other."

Someday, Launcelot Langstaff, Will Wizard, Anthony

Evergreen, Jeremy and Pindar Cockloft would be older and grow sober. William Irving was to serve New York in Congress from 1814 to 1819. James Kirke Paulding would be a well-known novelist and Martin Van Buren's Secretary of the Navy. Washington Irving would be almost deified and Sunnyside visited as a shrine. The time was not yet. William Irving was writing the sentimental and humorous verse in *Salmagundi.* Paulding was writing the pseudo-oriental pieces by Mustapha Rub-a-Dub Keli Khan. Washington Irving was writing most of the rest of the urbane, witty, polished papers that poked fun at Gotham—the three were the first to call New York "Gotham"—providing a glorious frolic for both writers and readers.

One piece, February 24, 1807, even poked fun at the kind of writer Irving was to become in *The Sketch Book, Bracebridge Hall,* and *Tales of a Traveller.*

> Perhaps there is no class of men to which the curious and literary are more indebted than travellers;—I mean travel-mongers, who write whole volumes about themselves, their horses and their servants, interspersed with anecdotes of innkeepers,—droll sayings of stage-drivers, and interesting memoirs of —the Lord knows who.

There were other portents of things to come. One number of *Salmagundi* talked of a headless horseman.

chapter IV

New York was pushing the 100,000 mark. People ridiculed the planning commission which had laid out streets in the wilderness as far north as 155th Street, but the city had reached Canal Street, which actually had a canal running through it in those years. The botanical gardens of Dr. David Hosack of Columbia were three miles outside the city, an estate on the middle road between Bloomingdale and Kingsbridge. Rockefeller Center stands there now on ground which still belongs to Columbia University.

The rich and successful, mercantile families like the Irvings, still lived at the lower end of Manhattan. Rusty oil lamps lighted the streets at night and constables in voluminous capes and leather caps kept watch. Pigs roamed the streets during the day, eating refuse tossed from the houses. Philadelphia and Boston newspapers often ridiculed New York's first primitive but efficient street-cleaning department.

This was the city which made *Salmagundi* the talk of the town. As many as 800 a day of some issues were sold. In an early advertisement the authors had tried to puff their "good-natured raillery." This appeared in print as "good-natured villainy." Paulding and the two Irvings liked the improved phrase better and adopted it. New York applauded their villainy.

The publisher of *Salmagundi* was a theatrical printer named Longworth. He was as eccentric a character as any in Cockloft Hall. He called his shop "The Sentimental Epicure's Ordinary" and had a large painting of the crowning of Shakespeare painted on the outside of it. Longworth suggested that the three authors copyright *Salmagundi.* Young gentlemen who considered literature an elegant accomplishment rather than a prosaic employment, they did not bother. As a result, Longworth made from $10,000 to $15,000 on *Salmagundi,* while Paulding and the two Irvings made about $100 each. What mattered to them was an appreciative public, and they had it. Washington Irving tasted the sweets of literary success, and he quickly wanted more.

He had traveled north to Quebec and covered much of Europe. Now he turned south. In Philadelphia he met and liked the wit, Addisonian essayist, and anti-Jeffersonian Joseph Dennie, editor of the *Port Folio.* He went to dances, dinners, and parties. He flirted gallantly and wrote back bantering letters—some of them almost coquettish—of his social successes.

In 1807, as a junior in the law office defending the accused traitor, Irving was sent to Richmond to cover the trial of Aaron Burr. Judge Hoffman did not think Irving would be of much help to Burr as a lawyer, but he had a vague notion that Irving might help his client in some literary way.

Irving enjoyed the spectacle. He reported admiringly that Burr took no notice in court of his chief accuser, General James Wilkinson, whom many thought had been in the conspiracy himself. Burr remained proud and imperturbable throughout the trial. Women, as they always did, found Burr charming. Irving admired that, too.

He visited Burr in his cold, newly-whitewashed prison cell, though Burr, already condemned in the public eye, was allowed no visitors. "I was permitted to enter for a few moments, as a special favor, contrary to orders . . . he was composed and collected as usual; but there was not the same cheerfulness that I have hitherto remarked. . . . I bid him farewell with a heavy heart, and he expressed with peculiar warmth and feeling his sense of the interest I had taken in his fate. I never felt in a more melancholy mood than when I rode from his solitary prison."

In later years Irving would sometimes take credit jestingly for Burr's acquittal. He did not really like Burr, but he did like feeling melancholy. Melancholy was at the time a fashionable literary pose which, when depressed, he had no trouble in adopting. There was little melancholy in the rest of his activities in Richmond and none in the letter he wrote Mary Fairlie. Mary Fairlie, a Philadelphia beauty who later married the actor Charles Cooper, had been the original "Sophie Sparkle" in *Salmagundi*.

With some complacency he wrote her, July 7, 1807, that he found he had in Richmond the reputation of being an *interesting young man*. He underlined the words. That reputation, like all fame, had its drawbacks.

> The tender-hearted fair ones think you absolutely at their command; they conclude that you must, of course, be fond of moonlight walks, and rides at day-break, and red-hot strolls in the middle of the day . . . and "melting-hot—hissing-hot" tea parties, and what is worse, they expect you to talk sentiment and act Romeo, and Sir Charles, and King Pepin all the while. 'Twas too much for me; had I been in love with any one of them, I believe I could have played the dying swain, as eloquently and foolishly as most men; but not having the good luck to be inspired by the tender passion, I found the slavery insupportable.

Richmond and Philadelphia were all right in their way, and in some ways considerably better than that, but what Washington Irving really wanted was to add to his literary reputation. This time it was Peter Irving, who had been abroad on family business, who joined him in a new venture.

They decided to burlesque a book which had just been published, Dr. Samuel Mitchell's *Picture of New York*. Added impetus was given their decision when they discovered how little most New Yorkers knew of the history of their city. The United States was young, but New York was already over 200 years old. It had a rich and varied history as a Dutch colony before it became an English possession and then an American metropolis. The brothers went to work. They did not work together long. Peter returned to England, and Washington Irving went to work alone with zeal and interest.

Earlier he had written lightheartedly and off the top of his mind. *Jonathan Oldstyle* and *Salmagundi* had been little more than the pleasant exercises of a ready pen. Like them, his comic history would be humorous. It would be spoof, but spoof with a serious base.

Irving read old books and consulted old records. He talked with old men who knew the city well and remembered tales they had been told when they were young. While he was in Philadelphia he wrote Henry Brevoort and asked him to copy down the inscription on Peter Stuyvesant's tombstone in the churchyard of St. Mark's on the Bouwerie. He talked with the elder Henry Brevoort.

Though Diedrich Knickerbocker's *History of New York*—which actually started Washington Irving on the road to fame—was as frivolous as his first published writings, it was really a scholarly work based on study and research. Working at it intently, Irving learned some of the library skills of the serious student which years later were to serve him in good stead.

He wanted to live up to his brothers' hopes for him and his for himself, and there was added incentive: he had fallen in love with seventeen-year-old Matilda Hoffman, Josiah Hoffman's daughter by his first wife.

Irving had long known her as a quiet child in the family. He seems suddenly to have become aware of her attractiveness and to have been deeply affected by her gentle character. He did not plan on an early or a hasty marriage. There was always a streak of practical caution in the romantic Washington Irving. In a letter he wrote, "I think these early and improvident marriages are too apt to break down the spirit and energy of a young man, and make him a hard-working, half-starving, repining animal all his days." He had no wish to be hard-working and half-starved, but he was carried away by his emotions.

As he put it himself, he went blindly along, happily along, like a boy in love. His exalted feelings added new exhilaration to his work on the book which he hoped would bring him reputation and perhaps the offer of a gentlemanly post in the public service.

The worst happened. Matilda caught cold. Her illness grew rapidly worse. It became what people then called "galloping consumption." Irving, who idolized and idealized his beloved, was stricken. He was at her bedside every day. "I saw her fade rapidly away; beautiful, and more beautiful, and more angelical to the very last." Matilda Hoffman died April 20, 1809. "I was the last one she looked upon."

Irving, now twenty-six, was tragic in his grief. He tried to continue work on his book but could not. He sought diversion in society and did not find it. He traveled into the country but could not endure the solitude. He tried to fall in love with other girls. He could not.

Irving suffered deeply through the loss of Matilda Hoffman, and the loss left its deep mark. He fell in love many times in later years, but he never married. It was not always the memory of Matilda that dissuaded. His habitual caution, the value he placed on his freedom of movement, possibly the rejection of his advances all helped keep him a bachelor. As it usually does, the anguish of his grief faded, but the memory of Matilda Hoffman remained. He kept her Bible and prayer book with him always and at his death was found to be wearing a locket containing a miniature of her and a lock of her hair.

He had to force some of the humor which had come so easily before, but gradually Irving was able to work again on his book. Finished at Ravenswood, a country retreat near Hell Gate where Long Island Sound empties into the East River, it was ready for the press only a few months after Matilda Hoffman's death. The public had known about it weeks before and was waiting for it.

The Irvings engineered a series of advertisements which began to appear in the newspapers in October 1809. The first, headlined "Distressing," begged for any news of "a small elderly gentleman, dressed in an old black coat and cocked hat, by the name of KNICKERBOCKER" who had disappeared from his lodgings. "As there are some reasons for believing he is not entirely in his right mind," the *Evening Post* or the Columbian Hotel on Mulberry Street would welcome word of him.

On November 6 the *Evening Post* reported that a traveler had glimpsed an old man resting by the side of the King's Bridge who answered the description. He had a bundle tied in a red bandanna.

Ten days later this letter appeared in the newspaper.

> *To the Editor of the Evening Post*
>
> Sir:—You have been good enough to publish in your paper a paragraph about Mr. Diedrich Knickerbocker, who was missing so strangely from his

lodgings some time since . . . but a *very curious kind of a written book* has been found in his room in his own handwriting. Now I wish you to notice him, if he is still alive, that if he does not return and pay off his bill, for boarding and lodging, I shall have to dispose of his Book, to satisfy me for the same.

I am, sir, your humble servant,
Seth Handaside
Landlord of the Independent Columbian Hotel,
Mulberry Street.

Handaside and his wife admitted in other advertisements that they had discovered the tattered and blotted manuscript in the saddlebags of their vanished lodger, who had told them that the bags contained his treasure.

So perturbed was one city official by what he read that he approached John Irving about the propriety of offering a reward for the discovery of the aged Diedrich Knickerbocker. He was never found. Accordingly, December 6, 1809, Inskeep & Bradford published *A History of New York from the Beginning of the World to the End of the Dutch Dynasty* by Diedrich Knickerbocker. The publishers declared, "This work was found in the chamber of Mr. Diedrich Knickerbocker, the old gentleman whose sudden and mysterious disappearance has been noticed. It is published to discharge certain debts he has left behind."

The teaser campaign worked. The book, for which Washington Irving received about $3,000, was an instant success. It deserved to be. The history was factual enough, but the treatment was hilarious. The Dutch were twitted and tweaked through all the long history of Nieuw Amsterdam. Dignified old Dutch worthies were transformed into figures of fun in the first really comic American book.

Solemn descendants of old New York families who felt that their ancestors had been treated with appalling irreverence were quite correct. Some of them never fully forgave Washington Irving. His satire was insistent and sometimes almost slapstick. The early heroes of New York came out somewhat less heroic, but certainly they came out vividly.

By edict of Hendrick Hudson, so Irving said, the old Dutchmen were limited to wearing only five pairs of pantaloons at one time. Irving knocked the pins from under Peter Stuyvesant—really only one pin, for the doughty governor wore a wooden leg. He lopped the heads off Peter the Headstrong and Wouter Van Twiller, whom he dubbed Walter the Doubter, and Wilhelmus Kieft, whom he called William the Testy.

Irving jibed and jabbed at the old Dutch settlers, but he was fair. He pinpricked himself, too.

> To a profound philosopher like myself, who am apt to see clear through a subject, where the penetration of ordinary people extends but half-way, there is no fact more simple and manifest than that the death of a great man is a matter of very little importance.

Irving suggested that the shrewd Dutch always got the best of it in their trading with the Indians. They were always strictly honest except that in weighing furs they maneuvered their hands and feet cleverly in the scales. Oloffe Van Kortlandt was "one of those infallible prophets who always predict events after they have come to pass."

Ten Broeck (Irving translated this into Ten Breeches or Tin Breeches) was "a poor but merry rogue." This, he said, was merely a casual remark which he would not for the universe have it thought he meant to apply to Governor Wouter Van Twiller.

> There are two opposite ways by which some men get into notice—one by talking a vast deal and thinking a little, and the other by holding their tongues, and not thinking at all. By the first many a vapouring, superficial pretender acquires the reputation of a man of quick parts—by the other, many a vacant dunderpate, like the owl, the stupidest of birds, comes to be complimented by a discerning world with all the attributes of wisdom.

Peter Stuyvesant was "a tough, sturdy, valiant, weather-beaten, mettlesome, obstinate, leathern-sided, lion-hearted, generous-spirited old governor." Irving was fairly kind to the one-legged hero, but hardly as kind to his subjects, "those fat, somniferous, respectable families that had flourished and slumbered away under the easy reign of Walter the Doubter."

Contemporary members of these families would gladly have lopped off Washington Irving's head. They refrained. There was an actual Knickerbocker family among the original Dutch colonists which rose to eminence in the city and the state. Herman Knickerbocker, a lawyer and a Congressman, became one of Irving's friends. In Washington he introduced him to President James Madison as "my cousin Diedrich Knickerbocker, the great historian of New York."

It was not through this family, though, but through Irving's history that the name Knickerbocker became well known in New York and that "Father Knickerbocker" became almost as familiar a cartoon character as "Uncle Sam" or "John Bull." Almost forty years after he had written his book, Irving proudly listed all the Knickerbocker societies, insurance companies, steamboats, hotels, and the rest that had been named for the fictitious historian he created. There are scores of Knickerbockers listed in the New York telephone book now. Washington Irving put them there.

Literary New York and Philadelphia rose and called Washington Irving their own. The Nine Worthies had to share their hero with the Renwicks, the Brevoorts, the Rhinelanders, the Astors, and all the rest of New York society. Irving left the parental home and took lodgings on Broadway near Bowling Green with his friend Henry Brevoort. He became more and more the young man of leisure and fashion. He made a gay trip to Philadelphia with Mrs. Hoffman and the Hoffman children. He no longer even pretended to practice law but, respectably, was in business with two of his brothers.

Peter and Ebenezer organized an importing company which bought goods in England and sold them in New York. Peter, who conducted the business in England, got two-fifths of the profits. Ebenezer, who ran it in Manhattan, got two-fifths. Washington Irving, who did nothing at all, got one-fifth. If ever he became active in the business or married, his share would be increased. It was a very pleasant working arrangement.

In 1811 he made a trip that was more in the nature of a fringe benefit than a workaday assignment. Congress had passed some measures considered injurious to business, and the brothers sent Washington Irving to Washington to lobby for their interests.

It took him a long time to get there. He stopped to socialize and be lionized in Philadelphia. After some days there, he stopped in Baltimore for more of the same. When he reached Washington he followed the program he had found so satisfactory in Philadelphia and Baltimore.

He dined with celebrities, wined with celebrities, danced with the wives and daughters of celebrities. He met Albert Gallatin and John Randolph of Roanoke. He visited at the White House and met Dolly Madison. Everywhere he went he was as popular as he was pleased and flattered. Always a genial companion, he was the more acceptable to Congressmen because he had no strong political convictions and did not take sides on controversial issues. He formed, as he wrote, a great number of "intimate and agreeable acquaintances," many of them useful. His name was proposed for the secretaryship of the American legation in Paris, but Joel Barlow, then minister to France, turned it down. This seems to have been the first of the many, many times that his friends sought public office for Irving.

Henry Brevoort went abroad in 1811. In England he placed copies of *A History of New York* in the hands of important people who might thus be brought to notice his friend's talents. When he was attending a series of lectures at Edinburgh University in Scotland, he met that city's powerful circle of writers and critics and saw to it that they also came to know the book. It was in this way that Walter Scott first read the Knickerbocker history.

Meanwhile its author was repining in New York. His

bright Washington interlude over, Irving was, for a little time, actually at work. On May 15, 1811, he wrote plaintively to Brevoort:

> Since you left us, I have been a mere animal; working among hardware & cutlery. We have been moving the store, & I (my pen weeps at the very thought of it) have had, in this time of hurry and confusion, to lend all the assistance in my power, and bend my indolent & restive habits, to the plodding routine of traffic. . . . By all the martyrs of Grubstreet, I'd sooner live in a garret, & starve into the bargain, than follow so sordid, dusty, soul killing a way of life; though certain it would make me rich as old Croesus, or John Jacob Astor himself.

It is the only time on record when Irving stooped to such menial tasks. Even then, as Brevoort well knew, he was not too put upon.

Irving was well looked after in their bachelor apartment. He was well mounted when he went abroad. In another letter he wrote, "My horse is doing well & according to Patrick's accounts eats his oats like a Gentleman." He envied Brevoort his travels and declared that if he were not fortunate enough to get happily married—he had been teasing his friend archly about mentioning "a fair Julia" in his sleep—he would console himself by "ranging a little about the world." He was consoling himself meanwhile at parties and by mingling that summer with the fashionable Gracies and Rhinelanders on their estates in the country about Hell Gate.

Soon Irving had regular occupation, which, if not completely to his taste, was better than wrestling with kegs of nails. In December 1812 he accepted the editorship of the Philadelphia *Select Reviews* at an annual salary of $1,200. He changed the name of the periodical to the *Analectic Magazine* and for a year worked conscientiously at his job. He wrote a biography of Thomas Campbell, the Scottish poet whom he admired, for his magazine and published the best contributions he could obtain, but, like most original writers, he disliked editing and writing criticisms of other peoples' books. Also, being Irving, he disliked being tied down to routine duties. He felt chagrin when the *Analectic* failed but relief at regaining his freedom. Never again would he accept a proffered editorial post.

More exciting diversion offered. Like other Americans he was embittered when the British sacked and burned Washington during the War of 1812. Ebenezer was already serving as a militia officer. Irving volunteered his services in August 1814. Typically, he started army life as a full colonel. As Colonel Washington Irving of the "Iron Greys" of the New York State Militia he became aide-de-camp and military secretary to Governor Daniel D. Tompkins who had taken to the field as major-general of his state's forces. For four busy months Irving attended meetings in Albany, wrote orders for Tompkins' signature, served generally as an efficient staff officer, and dashed about in uniform on horseback. When Tompkins relinquished field command and returned to his gubernatorial desk, Irving was discharged. He thought of going to Philadelphia to apply for a regular army commission, but his brothers dissuaded him.

He returned to New York from where he wrote Brevoort asking him to bring back more fashionable clothes from London and suggesting they move into better accommodations when he returned from Europe.

Irving liked businessmen if, like Brevoort and Astor, they were successful enough to enjoy the comforts and luxuries of life. He liked politicians and their ladies provided he did not have to battle in the muddy political arena. He liked writing that brought him reputation and admiration but did not entail his becoming a working writer. Industry was not one of the ideals of the Nine Worthies. Irving's ideal at this time seems to have been to be, and to be known as, a young man of the fashionable world of New York who wrote occasionally and elegantly. The delightful arrangement with Peter and Ebenezer obviated any undignified scratching for a living. Family affiliations and the reputation he had achieved first with *Salmagundi* and then the Knickerbocker history provided entree into the society he wished. Despite his literary ambitions, for six years after the publication of his first real book Irving seems to have made no serious effort to write another.

He was busy being pleasant and keeping himself pleasantly amused. His letters were light, careless, and carefree. They were full of gossip about who was engaged to whom or who might marry so-and-so. He wrote happily of voyaging up the Hudson with a bevy of "fair nymphs." He wrote of somebody's "divine Julia,—I suspect she has an alabaster heart in that fair bosom." He kept urging Brevoort that they get and furnish a handsome apartment as soon as he got home.

Sailing for England, May 1815

They did. They took commodious quarters in the home of a Mrs. Bradish at Rector and Greenwich Streets. A wine merchant, a Captain Porter, and others also lived in the house. So did Stephen Decatur and his wife. Irving became very friendly with the Decaturs.

Famed for his naval victories and personal heroism in the Tripolitan War, Decatur had fallen out of favor when he lost his ship, the *President*, to the British off Long Island. He was actually captured while on his way to New York to celebrate earlier victories over the enemy in the War of 1812.

Recovered from his wounds and vindicated by a board of inquiry, Decatur was now offered command of a squadron of nine ships sailing against the Dey of Algiers. He asked Irving's advice, and Irving urged his acceptance. He then invited Irving to sail aboard his frigate. Irving eagerly accepted, hastily packed his trunk, and had it sent aboard the commodore's flagship.

When Congress delayed sailing orders for the squadron, Irving had his trunk taken ashore again so as not to embarrass Decatur. Then, as long as he was all ready to travel, Irving, now thirty-two, decided to go abroad anyway. Peter was in England for the Irving firm. Their sister Sarah lived in Birmingham where she was married to the merchant Henry Van Wart. There were sufficient business and family reasons for him to indulge his restlessness through travel. Though he made no definite plans, he did not expect to stay abroad too long.

Washington Irving sailed for England May 25, 1815.

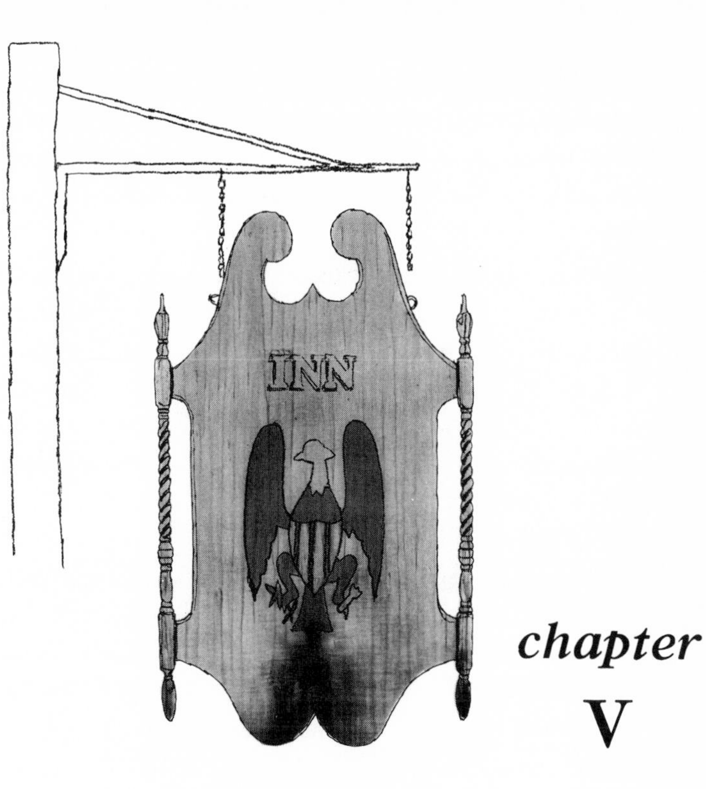

chapter V

Irving landed in an England still elated over Wellington's defeat of Napoleon at Waterloo the year before. The long wars were over. Europe was free of the fear of Napoleon's depredations. It was the beginning of a new and better era.

Irving knew all this. He even felt a little sorry for Napoleon, whom he considered "a noble fellow," but he had other and more immediate concerns. Peter was unwell, and the business was not thriving. Irving stayed with him in Liverpool for a short time, then went on to the Van Warts'. He was delighted with everything about the Birmingham household and the people in it, particularly the children with whom he romped. His pleasure there was cut short when Peter's continued illness and enforced absence from the ailing business made it necessary for someone else to take hold.

For several months he worked at what he always found the repugnant tasks of commerce, complaining bitterly all the time that the work wore him out and so disturbed him that he was unable to write. The War of 1812 and the British blockade had severely damaged American business, that of the Irvings along with all the rest. There was not much anyone, particularly someone as unskilled and inexperienced as Washington Irving, could do about it.

He managed to make little excursions about England with his sister. In Birmingham he played his flute, and his small nieces danced merrily to its music. Peter seemed to get no better. Neither did the business. The aftermath of the war was proving as disastrous as the war itself. A year went by, then most of another. Irving decided that he would go home, but the death of his mother in 1817 put an end to his chief reason for wanting to go. Then came the great event in one of the few unfortunate periods in the usually very fortunate life of Washington Irving.

In the summer of 1817, armed with a letter of introduction from Thomas Campbell, Irving called on Walter Scott at Abbotsford. Not yet knighted, Scott was famed as the author of *The Lady of the Lake*, *Marmion*, and his other narrative poems. He had not yet acknowledged authorship of the Waverley novels but was well known to have written them. Abbotsford was not yet the pretentious medieval pile he made it but the modest rural retreat of an Edinburgh writer, publisher, and man of affairs.

Scott and his family were at breakfast when Irving sent the postilion in with his card. Tall and powerfully made, Scott called out a greeting and limped up the hill to Irving's carriage to greet his visitor. He insisted that Irving join him, his wife, his two teen-age daughters, and his two young sons at the table. "Hout, man, a ride in the morning in the keen air of the Scotch hills is warrant enough for a second breakfast!"

Irving had already met Scott's Edinburgh intimates: Francis Jeffrey, the feared critic; Dugald Stewart, the influential philosopher; and the others. He knew all of Scott's work well. Thanks to Brevoort, Scott had read *A History of New York* and reveled in its humor. He thought and said that its young author was a writer of great promise. Always generous and open-hearted, Scott—a hero to the romantic Irving—insisted now that Irving spend several days with him at Abbotsford.

Scott in an old green hunting jacket with a dog whistle in the lapel and always dogs at his heels, the two men walked the countryside. Irving listened eagerly as Scott talked of books, people, characters of the Border country, old tales, old ballads. He sent his son Charles, then eleven or twelve years old, to show Irving around Melrose Abbey. From a hilltop, the host showed his enraptured guest Lammermuir, Smalholme, Galashiels and Gallawater, Teviotdale, the Braes of Yarrow; all places he had celebrated in his writing. The proofs of *Rob Roy* had arrived, and Irving saw them about the house, but Scott did not mention them. He never spoke of his writing in the presence of his children.

At dinner, Scott, dressed in black, held forth with anecdote after anecdote. The two girls wore sprigs of heather in their hair. A stag hound and a spaniel waited for bits from the table. A large gray cat slept always in Scott's bedroom. Scott kept a human skull there, probably that of an old friar, and sometimes horrified the maids by leaving his necktie draped around it. Irving was entranced by every detail of all he saw and heard, and remembered it all vividly.

Years later he wrote, "When I retired for the night, I found it impossible to sleep; the idea of being under the roof of Scott, of being on the borders of the Tweed, in the very centre of that region which had for some time past been the favorite scene of romantic fiction, and above all the recollection of the ramble I had taken, the company in which I had taken it, and the conversation which had passed, all fermented in my mind, and nearly drove sleep from my pillow."

In Scott's library and study were corselets of mail, battle-axes, gauntlets, broadswords, guns. Scott read to Irving one night from an old manuscript. Dogs listened at his feet, but it was his cat Scott remarked. He said that he always treated it kindly, as it might be a great prince in disguise.

In a day when conversation was valued, Scott's was magnificent. His humor was part of it. On their walks he introduced Irving to the simple people who were his country neighbors. They loved him, and he returned their affection. "The character of a nation is not to be learnt from its fine folks," he told Irving. He urged him to study German, to read the old German stories, to use tales and legends in his writing, and Irving listened intently.

One day Irving mentioned Scott's children pleasantly,

and Scott grew serious. "They have kind hearts, and that is the main point as to human happiness. They love one another, poor things, which is everything in domestic life. The best wish I can give you, my friend, is, that when you return to your own country you may get married, and have a family of young bairns about you. If you are happy, there they are to share your happiness—and if you are otherwise—there they are to comfort you."

Irving remembered and used the words in one of his essays, but he never followed Scott's advice. When Irving left, Scott urged him to return for a few more days after he had finished his planned tour of the Highlands, or to come whenever he pleased. He would always be welcome at Abbotsford.

The influence on Irving of this meeting with Scott was deep and lasting. He owed much all the rest of his career to Scott's encouragement, to his example, to his advice, and, only a few years later, to his practical help.

The Irving business in England went into bankruptcy early in 1818.

Irving felt humiliated and depressed. Following Scott's advice, he was studying German, but he could not concentrate. He went with his sister, who was unwell at the time, to Leamington, a few miles from Birmingham. He felt unwell enough himself. The failure was a shock. Irving had always had financial security and assumed its continuance. Suddenly the source had vanished. He was not poverty-stricken. There was always money enough for him to live and travel as he wished. His straitened circumstances were only comparative. Irving found the situation distasteful and a little frightening, but he did not feel pushed enough to accept any mundane job, even when a lucrative one was offered.

William Irving, now in Congress, wrote him. Stephen Decatur had become a Naval Commissioner in Washington. He was holding open the job of first clerk of the Navy —really assistant secretary—for Washington Irving. His salary would be a splendid $2,400 a year.

Irving declined it. His reasons? "The principal one," he wrote, "is, that I do not wish to undertake any situation that must involve me in such a routine duties as to prevent my attending to literary pursuits." If he had to do anything at all, he would write for a living. He went to London.

His painter friend, Washington Allston, was leaving, but he had other artist friends there. Charles Leslie he had known in Philadelphia. He had met Stuart Newton, a nephew of Gilbert Stuart, in England. He had made other friends.

His first depression over, Irving went to work. He had his subject. His subject was England as it appeared to a fascinated American. It was also the remembered beauty of the Hudson valley and the tales and legends he had heard in the countryside about Tarrytown. He began to gather and note his impressions. Allston, Newton, and Leslie painted and sketched. Irving began to sketch too, but his sketches were in words on paper in his notebooks. What he saw, heard, read, and thought he jotted down to expand into stories and essays.

Washington Irving walked to walk, not to get somewhere. He ambled for the sheer pleasure of it. Equable, despite what he considered his misfortunes, imperturbable when he was not ill or acutely unhappy, he watched the passing scene in England and thought about England's past and the old Dutch villages along the Hudson. He was an observer and a reflective reporter, and what he observed and thought about whether he was in New York, Westchester, Birmingham, London, or an English country house over the Christmas holidays was the pageantry of life. For him it was pageantry because it was pageantry he looked for. He was the curious, mildly meditative spectator of the romantic and quaint in incident and character.

The gentle in life pleased Irving, the sweetly sad, and the quietly amusing. He liked old stories and liked to retell them in his own fashion. He was friendly with the memory of vanished highwaymen of the Robin Hood order, of knights in shining armor, of stalwart, fair-minded country squires and their honest tenants. He wrote of these in pure and limpid English. His style from the beginning was smooth, gentle, whimsical. It became more musical. His essay-stories were steeped in his own kindly humor and his relaxed contemplation.

On March 3, 1819, Washington Irving sent the first number of *The Sketch Book of Geoffrey Crayon, Gent.* to his brother Ebenezer for him to get it printed and placed on sale in the United States. The first number contained a prospectus, "The Author's Account of Himself," "The Voyage," "Roscoe," "The Wife,"—and "Rip Van Winkle." It was printed in New York by C. S. Van Winkle (no relative) in a pleasant-looking little book priced at seventy-five cents. It appeared at about the same time, May 15, 1819, in Boston, Baltimore, and Philadelphia.

In his prospectus Irving—who had been Jonathan Oldstyle, then Launcelot Langstaff, then Diedrich Knickerbocker, and was now Geoffrey Crayon—said that the small book was an experiment. If the public liked it, more sketches would be forthcoming. The writer had no settled abode. He was subject to interruptions, and he had had his share of misfortunes. His writing might fluctuate with his moods. He would treat sometimes of scenes before him, at other times of things imaginary, and at still other times of memories of his own country.

Behind *The Sketch Book* lay all that Washington Irving was and had become to this time. *A History of New York* seems a rude guffaw compared to this gentle smile. Irving was older, thirty-six. He had seen something of the world. He had lost Matilda Hoffman. He had suffered financial loss. All of this had affected him. He was remembering at a distance in time and place, remembering sharply but quietly. He was observing and reflecting with some maturity. The flippancy was gone. In its place were pace, poise, and dignity.

Inspiration played its part. He had been walking across Westminster Bridge in London telling old Tarrytown stories to Peter when he was seized with the idea for "The Legend of Sleepy Hollow." He hurried back to his lodgings and made notes for it. The next dark and foggy morning he began to write it by candlelight. Brom Bones first rode and panic-stricken Ichabod fled in London. That most American of all Irving's stories, the story that is now part of the American legend, "Rip Van Winkle," Irving wrote in the very English home of the Van Warts in Birmingham.

Readers have thought they found tender reminiscences of Matilda Hoffman in "Westminster Abby," "The Wife," and in "The Widow and Her Son." They are not wrong. Irving wrote this in the notebook he kept while he was writing *The Sketch Book*.

> I heard a soft & plaintive voice singing Angels ever bright & fair—my heart melted at the words I drew into a corner of the cathedral and covering my face with my hands drank in the exquisitely mournful sound. My heart felt as if it would melt within me—the recollection of Matilda—ever allied in my mind to all that is pure spiritual & seraphic in woman came stealing over my soul—I recalled all the scenes of our early attachment—of her gentleness—her purity—& her kind affection . . .
>
> . . . Oh Matilda where was the soul felt devotion the buoyancy the consciousness of worth & happiness that once seemed to lift me from the earth when our eyes interchanged silent but eloquent vows of affection and I seemed to imbibe a degree of virtue & purity by associating with all that was virtuous & pure—How innocent how gentle—how lovely was then my life—How it has changed since—what scenes have I gone through . . . what jarring collisions with the world—what heartless pleasures . . . Misfortunes have crushed me to the earth—the cares of the world have hurried through my heart & worn it bare—I feel like one withered up & blighted—broken heart is like a desert wherein can flourish no green thing . . .

By late twentieth-century tastes, this is overdone and almost florid. It is melodramatic and overly sentimental.

It is the effusion of a man overwrought. It is the emotion of a few moments indulged without restraint, and it is not without self-pity, but there is anguish in what Irving wrote for only himself to read. There is poignancy. The man who wrote this felt it, and his feelings show in *The Sketch Book.*

The reviews when it appeared were ecstatic. Washington Irving was hailed as a genius. He was an American Addison. He was one of the world's finest writers, and he was an American. There was fierce patriotic pride in his accomplishment as well as joyous acceptance of the book.

Irving sent succeeding numbers to his brother and to Henry Brevoort to see through the printer's in New York. John, Edward, William, Ebenezer, and Brevoort (who was also taking care of the accounts) were all correcting proof.

Heartened and happy, Irving was still apologizing for not taking the proffered navy job in Washington but confirmed in his ambition. On July 10, 1819, he wrote Brevoort, ". . . I should have been perfectly out of my element and uncomfortable in Washington. . . . My mode of life has unfortunately been such as to render me unfit for almost any useful purpose . . . My acquirements, tastes, and habits are just such as to adapt me for the kind of literary exertions I contemplate. It is only in this way I have any chance of acquiring real reputation, and I am desirous of giving it a fair trial."

At first Irving had not intended to publish *The Sketch Book* in England, but some numbers recrossed the Atlantic. A London publisher was planning to collect and issue the essays and stories from American sources without payment to the author. To protect himself, Irving offered the manuscript for publication to the well-known English publisher, John Murray. Murray turned it down. Irving turned to Scott for help. Enthusiastic about the book and about Irving, Scott not only saw to it that, after some initial complications, *The Sketch Book* was well and profitably published in England, but also offered Irving the editorship of a literary magazine about to be set up in Edinburgh.

Irving was glad to accept Scott's help, through which Murray took the book after the publisher John Miller who put out the first volume at Irving's expense failed, but he turned down the editorship. He did not need it.

Suddenly the writer who had been so despondent the year before found himself in possession of the best of two worlds.

Americans loved *The Sketch Book* because Irving had proved that the country was capable of producing an author of the first order. They loved "Rip Van Winkle" and "The Legend of Sleepy Hollow," and even the descriptions of England and the English. Most Americans then had family ties with England. They might hate England for its oppression before the Revolution and for its depredations during the War of 1812, but from childhood they had heard homesick tales of "the Old Country."

Federalist literary society, of which Irving and his friends had been members in good standing, was Tory English in tastes, manners, and literary loyalties. The literati of New York and Philadelphia were delighted. As Irving said, he had been born and brought up in a new country, yet educated in the literature of an older one. His mind had been filled from childhood with the historical and poetical associations of Europe. "England is as classic ground to an American, as Italy is to an Englishman." There were many in America who felt as Irving did. He spoke for them and to them.

When it was published in London, England took to *The Sketch Book* with eager amazement. Here was an American who understood and appreciated England and her traditions. Accustomed to thinking of the United States as a rude land of rough people living in mud huts surrounded by Indians and bad manners, England was astounded by Irving's polished prose. English readers were surprised, and they were flattered.

"It has been a matter of marvel," Irving wrote, "to my European readers, that a man from the wilds of America should express himself in tolerable English. I was looked upon as something new and strange in literature; a kind of demi-savage, with a feather in his hand instead of on his head; and there was a curiosity to hear what such a being had to say about civilized society."

The Sketch Book was the talk of London. Just three years earlier Irving had written Brevoort that he would not come home for at least another year. He did not want to see those he had left prosperous in adverse circumstances. He would have no means of support, and he did not want to be a bother to his friends. "If I must scuffle with poverty let me do it out of sight—where I am but little known . . ."

In 1820, Irving no longer had to fear poverty (or what he considered poverty). He was no longer little known.

He was as much acclaimed in England as in America, and it was more important acclaim. It came from famous writers and established literary critics. Scott loved *The Sketch Book*. His son-in-law, John Lockhart, enthused over it in print. Lord Byron praised it.

A hero to his own countrymen, Washington Irving, with his large dark eyes, husky voice, and winning smile, was the darling of English society.

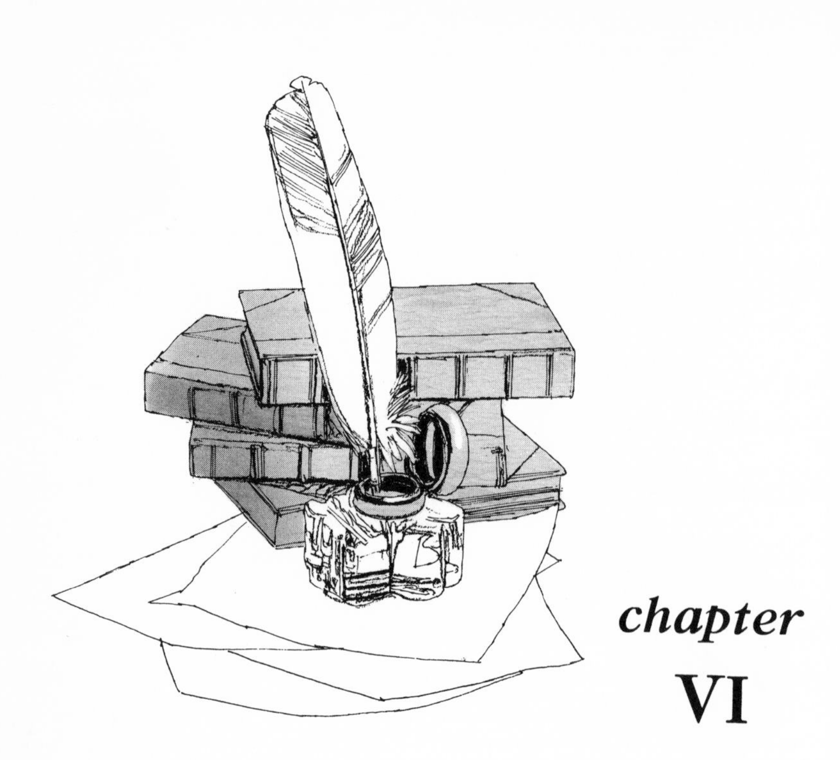

chapter VI

At his publisher's Irving met the outstanding contemporary writers. He came to know the Poet Laureate Robert Southey; Dean Milman, the editor of Gibbon; Henry Hallam, the historian; Isaac D'Israeli, the author whose son would also be a novelist as well as one of Queen Victoria's Prime Ministers. Irving met George Crabbe, clergyman and poet, became a close friend of the Irish poet, Thomas Moore. The poet Samuel Rogers was another friend. Lord Byron said he knew *The Sketch Book* by heart. In England Irving, as he said happily, was now "hand in glove with nobility and mobility."

The mobility took him on a visit to Paris where he

mingled with the historian George Bancroft, the American minister to France, Albert Gallatin, and other men of eminence. Modest always, Irving would not have been human had he not felt and expressed satisfaction in his accomplishment. He had no thought now of going home and every possible excuse for staying in Europe. As he wrote Henry Brevoort:

> I have by patient & persevering labour of my most uncertain pen, & by catching the gleams of sunshine in my cloudy mind, managed to open to myself an avenue to some degree of profit & reputation. I value it the more highly because it is entirely independent and self-created; and I must use my best endeavours to turn it to account. In remaining, therefore, abroad, I do it with the idea that I can best exert my talents, for the present, where I am, and that, I trust, will be admitted as a sufficient reply from a man who has but his talents to feed & clothe him.

Irving was being fed and clothed very well. As *The Sketch Book* grew in popularity, John Murray was giving him sums above those bargained for. Irving was on a ceaseless round of social activities and enjoying them to the full. He might fall asleep at dinner—an endearing habit for which he became famous—but he had his dinners, many of them. Of course, he had a few worries. He worried in 1820 about the costume in which he was being engraved in New York. He wanted his portrait when it appeared to be simple but picturesque, and, of course, in gentlemanly good taste.

He worried about Peter, who was seldom very well now. He and Peter were very close to each other. William had tried but failed to get Peter a high-salaried government post settling claims under a treaty with Spain. As a stopgap, Peter went to Bordeaux as agent for some London business houses.

Then what seemed to both Peter and Washington Irving a golden opportunity offered. Irving wrote William asking him to honor his note for $2,000 to invest in a steamboat line between Havre and Rouen on the Seine; he had already put up $5,000. Thinking the venture unwise, William refused. John Irving, who distrusted the venture, also refused. Irving was forced to appeal to the wealthy Brevoort for financial help. He understood that his older brothers had refused him out of kindness but complained to his friend that a man could be killed even by kindness. William and John were right. The scheme did not pay, but it gave Peter occupation. He went to Havre to manage the line.

By spring of 1821 Irving was in Paris with Thomas Moore, who had fled to France because of money judgments against him in England. Another friend, John Howard Payne, whom he had known as a precocious boy actor in New York, was in Paris for much the same reason. He had escaped from debtors' prison in London. Payne, who achieved fame with "Home, Sweet Home," which he wrote for the heroine to sing in his *Clari; or, the Maid of Milan*, had successfully written and produced other plays. A constant theatergoer, Irving was gripped with the idea of becoming a dramatist, and the two men collaborated. Because Payne could not return to England for fear of arrest, Irving tried to peddle his plays there. *Charles II* and *Richelieu*, two of the seven plays Irving and Payne wrote together, were briefly popular when Payne produced them in London a few years later, but Irving never rose to prominence as a playwright.

It was through Payne, also her admirer, that later Irving met Mary Wollstonecraft Shelley, twenty-eight-year-old widow of the poet, and is said to have fallen in love with her. In one of her letters she described Irving in Paris as "surrounded by fashion, rank, and splendid friendships."

Irving returned to England in the summer of 1821 in time for the coronation of George IV. After a tour of Derbyshire, he returned to Birmingham. At his sister's there he wrote from his notes *Bracebridge Hall; or, the Humorists*, a companion to *The Sketch Book.*

England had been kind to Irving. In this book he returned to the scene of his Christmas holidays in *The Sketch Book*, peopled Bracebridge Hall with the family, its connections, and its retainers, and wrote in greater detail and with even greater fondness of England. "Dolph Heyliger" and "The Storm Ship" in *Bracebridge Hall* are Diedrich Knickerbocker tales of Dutch New York. Some of the forty-nine stories and sketches in the book have French or Spanish settings, but most of *Bracebridge Hall* is about the country estate and events there. Irving wrote of hawking, falconry, horsemanship, love—of haunted houses and buried treasure, libraries, gypsies, the Tabard Inn—of old soldiers, the English character, forest trees. As Irving said it was, *Bracebridge Hall* is a medley of many elements. It is all Irving.

Sometimes he appears in his own character. "I traversed England, a grown-up child, delighted by every object, great and small; and betraying a wondering ignorance, and simple enjoyment, that provoked many a stare and a smile from my wiser and more experienced fellow-travellers." Sometimes Irving appears indirectly. It is the Squire talking to his sons in the essay on "Gentility," but there is no doubt that Irving approved his words and shared his ideal of the English gentleman.

> He should be a man at all points; simple, frank, courteous, intelligent, accomplished, and informed; upright, intrepid, and disinterested; one who can mingle among freemen . . . who can champion his country and its right either at home or abroad.

Irving heeded the squire's words. It was the ideal he seemed to follow abroad and at home, when he became a diplomat, and when he was master of Sunnyside.

Was this a sly reference to himself in "The Historian"? "I had all along maintained a quiet post at a corner of the table, where I had been able to indulge my humor undisturbed; listening attentively when the story was very good, and dozing a little when it was rather dull, which I consider the perfection of auditorship."

In "The Author's Farewell" at the end of *Bracebridge Hall*, Irving took leave of his book and of England as a subject. He knew that some would say he viewed England with too partial an eye. He alluded to the ill feeling in the United States caused by the attacks made upon it by the British press. He was convinced that a dormant good will really existed between the two countries and that "the liberal and enlightened" of the United States would "show themselves superior to the petty attacks of the ignorant and the worthless." He pled for amity between the two countries, though he said he left its promotion to others. He hoped that, at least, he had helped keep cordial sentiments alive.

"If I have, indeed, produced any such effect by my writings, it will be a soothing reflection to me, that for once, in the course of a rather negligent life, I have been useful; that for once, by the casual exercise of a pen which has been in general but too unprofitably employed, I have awakened a chord of sympathy between the land of my fathers and the dear land which gave me birth."

There is almost an affectation of Irving's characteristic modesty in this. He knew better than he wrote. He had done more to promote good feeling between England and the United States than any other writer had done or was apt to do. *The Sketch Book* and *Bracebridge Hall* had been no casual exercises of his pen but purposeful efforts to achieve reputation, and profitable both for Irving and his readers. His closing appreciative reference to the two countries was a calculated gesture to placate both. Irving always liked to insure good will and, if there were two sides to get it from, to get it from both.

Murray gave Irving a substantial present of books as well as a considerable sum of money for *Bracebridge Hall.* Irving immediately sent the books to his sister in Birmingham. He sent a copy of his new book to Ebenezer to arrange for its publication in the United States. He sent money to Peter in France, urging him to spend it for whatever he wished.

Early that winter of 1821 he suffered a hard blow. William Irving, businessman, poet, and capable public figure, always his youngest brother's benefactor, died at the age of fifty-six. Irving wrote Ebenezer that, though he had been prepared for it, "it was one of the dismallest blows that I have ever experienced." William, he said truly, had been a kind father to them all.

Bracebridge Hall made Irving more popular than ever in England. Parties, dinners, operas, balls, literary gatherings took up his days and nights. So many invitations poured in on him that friends began to weed them out so that he would skip the bores and waste no time on people who could do him no good. Eager as he always was to be in the swim of fashionable life, Irving found himself almost drowning in it.

He was tired from writing two major books in a short space of time. His ankles grew inflamed and the skin broke out. For five weeks in London he did not go out of doors except once, and that seemed to make him feel worse. Repeated treatments by various doctors seemed to do no good. Finally, feeling he knew as much as they about his mysterious but painful malady, Irving gave up his doctors, began to walk for exercise, and his health improved.

He grew restless. His rambling propensities took hold again. This time Irving had his health as excuse. On July 6, 1822, he left London for Holland and went from there to Aix-la-Chappelle to take the cure.

chapter VII

Scott had aroused Irving's curiosity about Germany and the Germans. Place and people, when he got there, delighted him. He began to travel about, to watch, to ask questions, to seek out odd characters, to note old legends and stories.

He responded to the beauty of the Rhine valley, which he compared to that of his native Hudson. He spent several days in medieval Heidelberg before he went on to Salzburg, Vienna, and Prague. He was not writing but soaking in the atmosphere, feeling his health return and his spirits rise as he viewed romantic scenery, thought romantic thoughts, and prosaically noted stories, places, people, and his own reactions for future use. He went on to Munich, then to Dresden, and here Irving spent some of the happiest months of his life.

Irving's fame had preceded him to the court of Frederick Augustus of Saxony. His books were known and relished there. He had met and mingled with nobility in England. Now he became the friend of petty royalty, and he loved it. Accepted at court, he became as well the intimate of Mrs. John Foster, daughter of Lord Carhampton, who was in Munich to educate her children, and of her family. Courted, flattered, made comfortable at the Fosters', Irving expanded in the warm and congenial environment. On Sunday, December 22, 1822, he made his debut and described the occasion in his notebook.

> Presented at court by Mr. Morier—presentation took place about twelve o'clock. First at Prince Antoine's apartments where I was presented to Prince Antoine and Prince Max, the king's brother. Then to Prince Max's sons, Prince Frederick and Prince John, then the Princess of Austria . . . the Princess Amelia of Bavaria . . . The Princess Amelia is a little of a blue stocking—spoke to me about my works—asked about America—our scenery, &c. Had been aboard one of our ships of war at Naples (probably the Franklin) and was much astonished at it.
>
> Princess of Bavaria very amiable, engaging countenance—much beauty—Prince John talked to me in English about my works . . .

All of this was important and gratifying to the hardware merchant's son from New York, the scion of a mercantile aristocracy who had always despised Thomas Jefferson and the Smellfungi.

Irving's notebooks filled with his jottings in Dresden. He had the inveterate writer's habit of putting down everything whether or not it could ever serve a useful literary purpose. He noted attendance at parties or theatrical performances, listed people he met and spoke with, noted what seem now, and what must often later have seemed to him, meaningless trivia. Sometimes, though, he scribbled cogent observations. In Dresden he wrote:

> Nations are fast losing their nationality. The great and interested intercourse, the exchange of fashions, the uniformity of opinions, the diffusions of literature are fast destroying those peculiarities that formerly prevailed. We shall in time grow to be very much one people unless a return to barbarism force us again into clans.

An early internationalist, Washington Irving foreshadowed almost a century and a half ago the international attitude fostered by such institutions as the United Nations. Both Irving and today's idealists and world planners seem to have discounted prematurely the toughness of geographic and emotional nationalism.

Irving was still studying German, the language and the literature. He was preparing to write a book on Germany, but much of his time was too pleasantly taken up with the entertainment offered by the friendly little court and his life in the Foster family circle.

One Sunday morning, October 13, 1822, there was a fete in honor of the king. The town was bustling with people in their best clothes crowding the streets. From his window facing the city square Irving could see them pouring out of the cathedral where they had been attending Mass. He saw the house next door was locked; his neighbors, the women and children brightly arrayed, had all gone to share in the excitement. It was too much for Irving. He locked his door behind him, shoved the key into his pocket, and went off to see the show.

He had a comfortable bedroom and sitting room on the first floor of a hotel on the square at 36 shillings a month. He said he wished to heaven he could get such quarters in London for anything like the price, but he had his complaints. He felt the bill for his food was extortionate and told his landlord so. The man explained that he had to pay dearly in the market for pheasant and other game. Irving believed he lied and made a note for future reference: "N.B. Dirty inns always dear."

Irving dined often at the royal table. He went hunting with the king. He attended many court ceremonies. He went often to the theater, usually stopping in afterward at Mrs. Foster's to sit and talk, sometimes into the early morning. The daughter, Emily Foster, was one of the attractions. It has been conjectured that Irving fell in love with her, proposed marriage, and was rejected. Pierre Munro Irving goes to great length in his life of his uncle to deny that there was any truth in this, but the evidence seems to say that there was. It was for the Fosters that Irving, who never mentioned his early love and disappointment to anyone else, wrote a long explanation of why he was unmarried, telling in detail of his first love for Matilda Hoffman.

Irving not only went to the theater in Dresden, he also

played at theater. Private theatricals with the Fosters and other friends were part of his happiness that winter and spring. He played Sir Charles Rackett in *Three Weeks After Marriage* to what, he modestly admitted, was great applause. He no longer ate honey cake offstage. Mrs. Foster helping, he was busy all one day getting dressed for the part of Don Felix in *The Wonder*. The "wonder" was that a woman could keep a secret.

For this part Irving had to have a pistol. When he got one, he found it was loaded so he fired it out of his window. This was against the law, and the prescribed punishment was a fine of $20 and confiscation of the weapon. Irving was let off with a fine of $2 and allowed to keep his pistol. It paid to know the king.

He was surprised at the discovery of his hitherto unsuspected dramatic talent and declared that, if the worse came to the worst, he could turn strolling player. Irving was gay in Dresden and popular. Witty and humorous in easy-flowing conversation, he was welcomed into the inner circle of royal and patrician society, yet, for whatever reason, darker moods sometimes overcame him. "Monday the 14th—Take lesson early—endeavour to write poetry, but in vain—wrote only one verse—determine not to dine today at Mrs. Foster's. Go to Mrs. Foster's —take Italian lesson—Emily somewhat better—very pale —leave there about 4—Mrs. Foster very urgent for me to stay—return home but do not dine—go to theatre—see a German comedy—rather amusing—sit in Baron Lowenstein's box."

Perhaps depressed by Emily Foster's rejection, further depressed because he had not been writing, Irving returned to Paris. There he was with old friends again. A library, from which he could borrow as he pleased, was only a five-minute walk away. He began to work at plays again with Howard Payne. Peter joined him in bachelor apartments. He got started on one new book, abandoned it, and under urging from Murray and William Gifford, editor of the *Quarterly Review*, wrote his *Tales of a Traveller*.

In a way, the new book by Geoffrey Crayon, Gent., was Irving's book about Germany. Resembling *The Sketch Book* and *Bracebridge Hall* in form, it drew on German and European background for "Strange Stories by a Nervous Gentleman," a group of nine stories, and for "Buckthorne and His Friends," ten more tales which made up part two of the book. Part Three was more tales, "The Italian Banditti," and the last part of the book ("found among the papers of Diedrich Knickerbocker," a useful device on which Irving had depended ever since *A History of New York*) dealt humorously with the life, adventures, and buried treasure of Captain William Kidd.

Irving delivered the manuscript in person to Murray in London in May 1824. Then, by way of recreation after labor, joined his friend Moore in Bath and then went on to Moore's home. Irving was very much at ease with Moore. His friend found him full of fun and drollery. He visited in Birmingham, where he was always happy in the Van Wart home.

The reception accorded *Tales of a Traveller* by the critics both in London and New York jolted him out of his contentment. The *Traveller* did not have the built-in appeal of *The Sketch Book* and *Bracebridge Hall*. It did not warm the English with appreciation for England's virtues by an American, and it did not titillate Americans with nostalgia for England. It was just another miscellaneous collection of indifferent tales, and the Diedrich Knickerbocker humor had staled. The lion of literary fashion was beginning to shed a little.

Reviewers condemned the *Traveller*. Many of them contrasted the new book unfavorably with Irving's earlier books. Some were savage.

Always anxious to please, Irving was deeply wounded. He resolved to have done with the short story and with his attempts at drama. Knowing his limitations, he knew he could not attempt longer fiction in the novel. He had always been able to write only when he could, not when he would. Monetary loss through bad investment did not help to cheer him.

There was worse. An anonymous "friend" in the United States kept writing him in Paris and sending him unpleasant comments from the American newspapers. Unfriendly critics were now accusing Irving of lack of patriotism, of toadying to the rich and well-placed in Europe, of abandoning staunch American principles. His vicious correspondent assured him helpfully that there had been violent demonstrations against him in the United States.

Friends tried to relieve Irving's despondency. They pointed sensibly to the ugliness of such cowardly anonymous attacks. They told him they were inspired only by envy and spleen. Irving could not be cheered. He confessed that it was ten times more important to him to be liked than to be admired. He hungered for the continuing affection of his countrymen.

Irving was so bitterly discouraged that he warned a nephew, Pierre Paris Irving, who was Ebenezer's son, against the ambitions which threatened to make him follow him into "the seductive but treacherous paths of literature." Depressed by the malignity of his anonymous attacker and by the ill reception of the *Traveller*, he wrote his nephew that he had "a thousand times regretted that ever I was led away by my imagination. Believe me, the man who earns his bread by the sweat of his brow, eats oftener a sweeter morsel, however coarse, than he who procures it by the labour of his brains."

The Edinburgh publisher, Archibald Constable, friend of Scott, was asking Irving for the life of George Washington which Irving had long intended to write. Murray in London was pressing for new work. Irving could not comply. He took stock of himself. As so often, he turned to Henry Brevoort. On December 11, 1824, he wrote him a long letter which contains the fullest account of his attitude toward his work that Irving ever wrote. It was, in effect, Washington Irving's literary credo.

> I fancy much that I value myself upon in writing escapes the observation of the great mass of my readers, who are intent more upon the story than the way in which it is told. For my part, I consider a story merely as a frame on which to stretch my materials. It is the play of thought, and sentiment, and language; the weaving in of characters lightly, yet expressively, delineated; the familiar and faithful exhibition of scenes in common life; and the half-concealed vein of humor that is often playing through the whole;—these are among what I aim

> at, and upon which I felicitate myself in proportion as I think I succeed. I have preferred adopting the mode of sketches and short tales rather than long works, because I choose to take a line of writing peculiar to myself, rather than fall into the manner or school of any other writer; and there is a constant activity of thought and a nicety of execution required in writings of the kind, more than the world appears to imagine. It is comparatively easy to swell a story to any size when you have once the scheme and the characters in your mind; the mere interest of the story, too, carries the reader on through pages and pages of careless writing, and the author may often be dull for half a volume at a time, if he has some striking scene at the end of it; but in these shorter writings, every page must have its merit. The author must be continually piquant; woe to him if he makes an awkward sentence or writes a stupid page; the critics are sure to pounce upon it. Yet if he succeed, the very variety and piquancy of his writings—nay, their very brevity, make them frequently recurred to, and when the mere interest of story is exhausted, he begins to get credit for his touches of pathos or humor; his points of wit or turns of language. . . . I believe the works that I have written will be oftener re-read than any novel of the size that I could have written. . . .

There is a touch of chagrin in what Irving wrote his old friend, but there is much more. *The Sketch Book*, *Bracebridge Hall*, and, to a lesser extent, the *Tales of a Traveller* were conscious works of art. Two succeeded superbly, the third not as well, but, stand or fall, they were deliberate creations. Their form, structure, and peculiar qualities were no accident. Irving's mix of humor, pathos, character, sentiment, and the style which blends them did not just happen. Washington Irving worked carefully with his tools and with his ingredients. Irving sometimes advertised his indolence too much. He worked at his writing. The seeming effortlessness of *The Sketch Book* was achieved through honest effort.

Irving was dissatisfied now in Paris. He had been abroad over ten years. He was forty-two years old. On January 12, 1826, he wrote Alexander H. Everett, United States minister to Spain. He reminded Everett of an earlier conversation and asked that he be attached to the American legation in Madrid. He made it clear that he did not wish to undertake routine duties. He wished most of his time free to write.

Brother of the more famous Edward Everett, Alexander Everett was a man of literary culture who later became editor of the renowned *North American Review* in Boston. He replied quickly and favorably, suggesting that Irving occupy himself in Spain by translating Navarette's *Los Viages de Colón* (*Voyages of Columbus*) which had recently been published.

Irving had been dreaming of Spain since childhood when he pored over *The World Displayed* in his father's library. He had been studying Spanish in Paris and reading Spanish history and literature. He had built his castles in Spain years before. He also knew that American interest in Spain was at its height. He would have a rich subject and a ready market.

Washington Irving reached Madrid in February 1826.

chapter VIII

At nineteen, Alexander Everett had been secretary to John Quincy Adams when Adams was American minister to Russia. Everett knew his way about the world, especially the diplomatic world. He was a scholar and a writer as well. He introduced his new attaché to life about the Spanish court and to the representatives of the other nations present there.

Irving then got a room for $5 a week in the home of Obadiah Rich, American consul to Valencia. Rich was a bibliophile who had gathered about him a matchless library of Spanish books and documents relating to the discovery and early settlement of the Americas. Irving had an understanding patron in Everett and in Rich a friend who placed his entire collection of Spanish source material at his disposal. Once more Irving had struck gold.

He soon found that Navarette's work was not suitable for translation. Quickly he turned to the wealth in Rich's library. He borrowed books from other libraries. He consulted manuscripts in the Spanish archives and soon was hard at work writing his own life of Columbus.

As everywhere he went, he made friends easily and quickly. In Madrid he became intimate with the Russian minister, Pierre D'Oubril, his pretty wife, their houseful of children, and particularly with the young and attractive niece of the minister's wife, Antoinette Bolviller. Often he rode in D'Oubril's ornate coach-and-four with the minister, his wife, and Antoinette. Many have scented another romance in Irving's attraction to Antoinette Bolviller.

With Prince Dimitri Ivanovitch Dolgorouki, secretary of the Russian legation, Irving formed a close and lasting friendship. Their tastes and talents were akin, and later they became traveling companions through Spain's mountain fastnesses. Irving also became close to Sir David Wilkie, the English painter, whom he made his companion in Madrid and whom he helped obtain lucrative commissions from the eminent and wealthy in Spain. Many of the nobility called to watch with Irving while Wilkie painted scenes from Spanish history for King George IV of England.

In contrast to his life in Paris, Irving's life in Spain was full and happy. His social life continued, but there was change in him. This time he was engrossed in a serious subject of very different kind from those he had treated in his earlier books. He strolled on the Prado with his friends of an evening. He went to the bullfights and enjoyed the pageantry and color. The slaughter of bulls and horses did not bother him unduly. He said he was surprised to find out how bloodthirsty he really was, and went as often as he could. He dined out. He went to the theater and the opera here as in London and Paris, but there was a difference. He was up early in the morning delving into old records, noting facts, checking them, and beginning to compose his story of Columbus.

Like most people, Irving was happiest when at work. His vaunted indolence had no place in his life now. Often he was up at four or five o'clock in the morning, and often he worked until late in the evening. The imaginative writer was still using his imagination—for Irving saw history as story and romance—but Irving had turned scholar. He had forsaken easy contemplation and leisurely writing for the demanding tasks of literary research, the painstaking checking of biographical and historical facts, then the forming of his discoveries into an informative and entertaining book.

Spain crystallized the forces in Irving. He reacted happily to scene, climate, the people about him, and to the task which fascinated. Purpose came into his writing. He was exerting all of his capabilities and directing them toward the end of solid literary and scholarly achievement.

Irving knew a new vigor. Day after day entries in his Spanish diary read: "write all day," "all day writing," "copy Ms.," "at library" (many times repeated). Sometimes he is disappointed in his accomplishment. He could not always maintain the pace he had set for himself: "incapable of work" appears often; "attempted to work . . . heavy & drowsy," "write a little . . . could not work freely."

Henry Wadsworth Longfellow, twenty-one years old and newly appointed professor of Romance Languages in Bowdoin College in Maine, from which he had graduated, had been staying in Paris with Irving's nephew. He called on Irving in 1827 when he came to Madrid. Irving was glad to see him, but he was not always free when the young professor called. "Sit down a minute," Irving would say. "I will talk with you in a moment, but I must first finish this sentence."

Longfellow saw Irving already at work when he passed his open window at six o'clock one morning. Irving told him he was always at work by that time. Thrilled by his nearness to a writer whose work he reverenced, Longfellow spent as much time with him as the busy Irving could manage. They walked the Prado together at night when it was cool. Longfellow found the man who was twenty-three years his senior "a fine man in society" and "all mirth and good humor." Before Longfellow left Madrid, Irving wrote letters of introduction for him to Sir Walter Scott and to five other men he thought might be helpful to the teacher and aspiring poet.

In Madrid, Irving wrote, "The capricious periods of the heat and glow of composition, have been the happiest hours of my life. I have never found in anything outside the four walls of my study, any enjoyment equal to sitting at my writing-desk with a clean page, a new theme, and a mind awake."

For a little while he got sidetracked from Columbus.

His researches led him into an even more fascinating epoch of Spanish history. The Moors, Mohammedans from North Africa, had invaded Spain early in the eighth century. They subdued the south of Spain and as time went on penetrated even beyond the Pyrenees. For more than 700 years they ruled in Spain, building a Moorish civilization on the Iberian Peninsula. The Moors had not been conquered and driven out of Spain until 1492, the year that Christopher Columbus discovered America.

Irving stopped work on Columbus long enough to sketch out a new book on the fall of Moorish Granada before the forces of Isabella of Castile. Then, almost reluctantly, he returned to finish his biography before he could work further on this period of Spanish history.

So rapt was Irving in what he was doing that he wrote Brevoort, "There is an independent delight in study and in the creative exercise of the pen . . ." He wished, he said, that he could just study and write, then lay aside the finished work and not let in "the noisy rabble of the world" by publication.

Irving may have meant what he said at the moment of saying it, but applause for his writing was the breath of life to him. He could not do without it. He wanted to write a book which would restore him to the esteem and affection of his countrymen which he feared he had lost. In February 1828, in another letter to Henry Brevoort, he wrote, "I confess it will give me satisfaction if my present work, by its success, replies to some of the cavilling that has been indulged against me . . ."

The Life and Voyages of Christopher Columbus did succeed. It brought Irving high praise and added reputation. It also brought him 3,000 golden guineas from John Murray in London.

Irving hardly hesitated in stride. Visiting the libraries every day, copying old manuscripts, writing at his table at Obadiah Rich's, he plunged into work on his Spanish history. When he had his preliminary research completed, he left Madrid to visit the scene in Granada.

His brother Peter, who had been staying with him, returned to Paris, as he was not well enough to endure the discomforts such travel entailed in 1828. It was in company with two friends from the Russian legation that Irving traveled by diligence and on muleback through mountainous country, infested for centuries by brigands, into Andalusia. An innkeeper was aghast when he saw them traveling with only two soldiers to protect them. He said the robbers could ambush them, shoot down their bodyguards, then—*"Buenas Noches!"*

The roads were narrow and twisting. They slept at some inns which were reputed to be the haunts of highwaymen. They met questionable characters, fared ill or badly as the day chanced, but they were not molested. Irving seeking out scenes of conflict between the Christians and the Moors as they moved along, they descended from the mountains to the plains and reached Granada. They visited the Alhambra, Irving returning alone later to explore the old Moorish palace and citadel by himself. Then he and his companions resumed their journey to Málaga, thence to Gibraltar. The journey took them a little over a month.

For several months Irving lived in Seville, working in the library of the cathedral and in the Archives of the

Indies. He became friendly there with a German scholar, Johann Nikolaus Böhl von Faber, and with his daughter who, as "Fernán Caballero," was just beginning to write her Spanish novels. Near Seville he finished his *Chronicle of the Conquest of Granada.* He sold it to Murray in London for £2,000, and Ebenezer got $4,750 for the book when it was published in New York.

It was a major work. Irving wrote history as Scott wrote novels. Scenes of carnage come out almost prettily. His warriors, Moors or Christian, were always manly and valiant. They cut off each other's heads gracefully. Irving's histories are stories that read rapidly, smoothly, and colorfully. The men are handsome; the women beautiful. Murder is motivated by the highest ideals. It was an age of chivalry about which Irving wrote, and he wrote of it chivalrously.

He reveled in the clash of scimitars, in the sun splashing off bright shields as knights rode their richly caparisoned steeds to the rescue of the good and the fair. He wrote accurately and honestly, but Irving wrote history as he saw it, and he saw it as splendor and romance. Sometimes he realized that battles were bloody, sackings merciless, the ravagings brutal—and he makes the reader share his realization—but, for the most part Irving, and the reader with him, are beglamored by the pageantry of medieval conflict. Bitter warfare becomes part fete, part tournament out of *Ivanhoe,* part grim history in Irving's *Conquest of Granada,* yet the book is one of substance. It was formidable achievement, and critics saw it as such.

On Wednesday, December 31, 1828, Irving was able to write in his diary with calm satisfaction:

> Thus ends the year—tranquilly. It has been one of much literary application, and, generally speaking one of the most tranquil in spirit of my whole life. The literary success of the History of Columbus has been greater than I anticipated and gives me hopes that I have executed something which may have greater duration than I anticipate for my works of mere imagination. I look forward without any very sanguine anticipations, but without the gloom which has sometimes oppressed me. The only future event from which I promise myself any extraordinary gratification is the return to my native country, which, I trust, will now soon take place.

The next spring Irving and Prince Dolgorouki set out on horseback from Seville to Granada. They hoped for the best but were prepared for the worst on this dangerous trek through the mountains. Like Irving, the prince was a seasoned traveler. Most moved along this route only in large and well-armed caravans. Their only escort was one combination groom, valet, and guard of about twenty, who might or might not know how to use the fearsome array of weapons he carried. Their chief precaution was to carry some hard cash by way of "robber purse." The wishful idea was that this might be enough to satisfy hijackers should they be attacked. There were dark reminders along the sides of the narrow and often precipitous passes: "ever and anon, the ominous cross, the monument of robbery and murder, erected on a mound of stones."

Despite the real perils, Dolgorouki and Irving rode into

Riding into Granada, Spring 1829

Granada intact. Irving saw not just the city before them but the city he had recreated from the past, the last stronghold of the Moor and the scene of Spanish triumph. It was a city surrounded by three leagues of high walls with twelve gates and thirty towers. On one hill stood the Alcazaba, a commanding fortress. On the other stood what Irving describes in the opening pages of his *Granada* as "the Alhambra, a royal palace and warrior castle, capable of containing within its alcazar and towers a garrison of forty thousand men; but possessing also its harem, the voluptuous abode of the Moorish monarchs, laid out with courts and gardens, fountains and baths, and stately halls, decorated in the most costly style of oriental luxury."

He and his companion went to the Alhambra—from a name meaning "the red castle" in Arabic. They went and they stayed. Apartments were maintained there for the governor of the province, but he preferred to stay in the city. He insisted that Irving and Dolgorouki use his quarters as they wished, and they accepted eagerly.

Irving was ecstatic. This was the Spain he had read of as a child. This was the Spanish past he had been writing about. The stately halls, the little gardens, the hundred old soldiers who guarded the palace, the aged retainers, the sunny skies of southern Spain—everything melted into a golden dream become blissful reality.

Dolgorouki moved on after a time. Irving stayed the whole enchanted summer. Chatelaine of the Alhambra was Doña Antonia, who did her best for the governor's guest. Her niece, plump, bright-eyed Dolores, kept Irving's room, made his bed, served his meals. She was engaged to Manuel Molina, who was studying medicine and hoped to become the Alhambra's doctor.

Mateo Ximénez, an odd youth who proudly dubbed himself a "son of the Alhambra," became Irving's guide, valet, and an inexhaustible source of the old legends and stories of the place that Irving sought. Mateo's aged father proved another font of ancient lore. An old woman whom Irving found in another part of the vast Alhambra had her tales to tell of the past. Irving made them all famous in his *Tales of the Alhambra* that he was soon writing in an old and ornate part of the palace.

In his explorations he had come upon rooms which had been fitted out by Italian artists for Queen Elizabeth of Farnese and the ladies of her court. To the dismay of Tía Antonia and his other faithful retainers, Irving insisted on moving from the governor's modern apartment into this remote royal suite. They were aghast, for they knew the rooms to be lonely and thought them probably haunted, but they helped him, and Irving moved into the heart of his castle in Spain.

In the silence and coolness of his sumptuous but decaying, thick-walled retreat Irving wrote down the tales he heard from Mateo and the others. The Duke of Gor lent him books and manuscripts from his curious library of old chronicles, and he read and noted them. Outside the windows of his queen's apartment were beautiful gardens. Granada lay far below him. Irving seldom went down into the city. He watched it through his spyglass when he turned from his work or in the evening.

The *Conquest of Granada* had come out of Irving's researches as he worked on his *Life and Voyages of Christopher Columbus*. His *Tales of the Alhambra* came out of his study and travel in writing *Granada*. Working on the stories, which he did not publish for several years, was pleasant relief from the hard inditing of his sterner histories. It was pleasurable relapse into his old penchant for tales and legends. This was Irving's Spanish *Sketch Book*, but it was more than that. It was warm expression of his delight in Spain.

The golden summer ended, and soon after Irving's three and a half years in Spain came to an end too. His friends at home had been at work on his behalf. Paulding and Jack Nicholson, a naval officer Irving had met (and got tipsy with) in Richmond at Burr's trial, had suggested to Martin Van Buren, then Secretary of State, that Irving be appointed secretary of the United States legation in London. After checking with John Treat Irving as to whether or not his brother would accept, Van Buren recommended Irving to President Andrew Jackson, who made the appointment.

Irving, now forty-six, was still in the Alhambra when notification reached him. He left reluctantly after prolonged and affectionate farewells to Dolores, Antonia, Mateo, and the others. Once again he took to the difficult roads of Spain. He delayed in Paris to spend a few days with Peter, but reached London early in October of 1829.

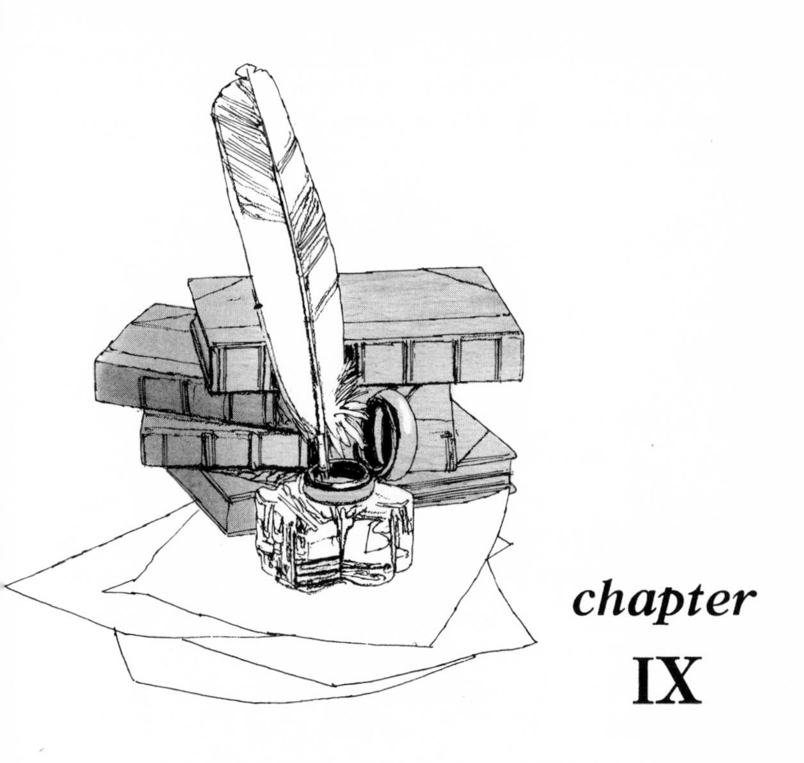

chapter IX

Irving had left London seven years before as the author of two particularly charming books. He returned with much more formidable biographical and historical writing to his credit and with new standing.

Columbia College had awarded him an honorary degree after the publication of *The Sketch Book.* Now, in recognition of his accomplishments, Spain made him a member of the Royal Academy of History in Madrid, a bright honor he shared with Sir Walter Scott. While cheering undergraduates shouted "Diedrich Knickerbocker!" and "Ichabod Crane!" Oxford solemnly conferred on Washington Irving its degree of Doctor of Laws.

The new secretary of the American legation was well known in England and capable and conscientious at his job. Thanks to his experiences in Spain, he knew something of diplomacy. He knew the routine duties of his post, and he knew statesmen and politicians and something of the European political situation. When the American minister, Louis McLane, was ill, Irving acted as head of the American legation. He earned his $2,000 a year.

He mingled much in society, dining out, attending balls and other functions at the Duke of Wellington's and the Duke of York's as well as receptions of the Queen. Lady Blessington, Lord Mahon, and the Duke of Sussex were among those he knew well. He talked often with King William IV. He made merry—or dozed—at informal dinners with Moore, Lockhart, Hallam, Sydney Smith. The demands of society were so great that Irving worried on one point. "I have a villainous propensity to grow round and robustious, and I fear the beef and pudding of England will complete the ruin of my figure," he wrote Gouverneur Morris.

He tried but failed to interest Murray in publishing the poems of William Cullen Bryant in England. Some years earlier, James Fenimore Cooper, who did not know him personally at the time, had asked his help in finding an English publisher for *The Spy* and *The Pioneers*, and Irving had done his best. He was always generous in trying to help other American writers. In 1828 he had refused Murray's offer of the editorship of his *Quarterly Review* because the *Review* had published too many articles hostile to the United States. Now he broke with Murray, who said he had lost money on *The Conquest of Granada*.

Irving talked with William Wordsworth, greatest of the English romantic poets. He visited Sulgrave Manor, ancestral home of George Washington, and deciphered the family monuments in the churchyard there. The rich and powerful Rothschilds invited him to Sunday dinner, but he could not accept as he was on his way to the Van Warts' home in Birmingham. He noted the details of another dinner in his diary.

> Dined at the anniversary of the Literary Fund—Prince Albert presided. I sat between Moore and Hallam, Bishop of Gloucester opposite and Mr. Everett—met Lockhart, Lord Mahon, Lord Lansdowne, Marquis of Northampton—James [G.P.R. James, English novelist]—Mr. Milne, etc—very nervous throughout the dinner, knowing my health was to be drunk. Sir Robert St. Inglis introduced it with a very warm and complimentary speech. It was cheered in the warmest manner, which contributed to embarrass me. Rose, declared my want of talent for public speaking, and returned thanks. After dinner James came up and shook hands with me cordially by way of resuming old acquaintance.
>
> At this dinner Campbell deputed to give Hallam's health. He made an introductory speech, but, having drunk too much wine, became so prosy and maudlin that he was absolutely clamoured down.

When Louis McLane returned to the United States to become a member of Jackson's cabinet, Irving stayed on in charge of the legation. Irving's friend Martin Van Buren was appointed minister to England in McLane's place, and, starting early, reached London late in the summer of 1831. Irving resigned as secretary September 20, 1831.

Before he left London he dined with Lockhart and Sir Walter Scott. It saddened Irving to see Scott old and worn, his mind failing. Peter came from France to join him, and the brothers went together to what for so long had seemed the family home in Birmingham.

Early in 1832 Irving traveled about England with Martin Van Buren, the immaculate little lawyer of Dutch ancestry from Kinderhook, New York, and Van Buren's son. They saw the countryside, visited homes and castles, and enjoyed each other's company for a month. When the Senate, by the deciding vote of John C. Calhoun, refused approval of Van Buren's appointment as minister, the Van Burens left to travel on the continent. Irving went on alone to Newstead Abbey, where he slept in Byron's bedroom and enjoyed strolling about Robin Hood's Sherwood Forest.

For a long time Irving had wanted to go home, but he had kept putting off his return. He wanted to see his brothers. He wanted to see New York. On April 2, 1832, Irving left London for Southampton. He crossed the English Channel to say goodbye to Peter at Havre, then sailed on the *Havre* April 12. On shipboard he met Charles Joseph Latrobe, English traveler and travel writer of thirty-one who would one day be governor of Australia, and the energetic young Count Albert Pourtales for whom he was acting as guide and companion. They proved good company.

On May 21, 1832, Washington Irving landed in New York. He had left it seventeen years before, mostly because his trunks were already packed and he had been disappointed in sailing with Stephen Decatur. He had been then one of the anonymous authors of *Salmagundi* who as "Diedrich Knickerbocker" had written an amusing history of his native city.

Nine days after his arrival home, Washington Irving, world-famous author, was hailed at a great public banquet in the City Hotel. Everybody who read at all read his books. Those who did not had heard of them and knew his name. "Rip Van Winkle" and "The Legend of Sleepy Hollow" were part of American folk history. Chancellor James Kent presided at the dinner which was attended by hundreds of New York's most eminent men.

Irving was greatly affected by the toasts and testimonials. They testified not only to his achievements as an author, but also to the esteem in which he was held by his countrymen. Always fearful of speaking in public, he spoke well and, being Irving, tactfully.

He quoted "This is my own, my native land . . ." from "The Lay of the Last Minstrel" by his old friend and patron, Sir Walter Scott. He said he had been led to suspect that his absence had impaired the kind feelings of his countrymen but had been too proud to defend himself against such vilification: ". . . the overpowering testimonials of regard here offered me . . . proved that my misgivings were groundless."

He had been asked, he said, whether he would be content to live in this country. "Whoever asks that question, must have but an inadequate idea of its blessings and delights." Happy as he had often been abroad, rapt as he had been in Spain, Irving sounds as if he must sometimes have been homesick. He had been asked, too, he said, how long he intended to remain in the United States. "I answer, as long as I live." He could not go on for the roared applause.

Irving was moved, and he was politic. He was also a little aghast. He was shocked at the forgotten rudeness of much in American life. In England, France, Germany, and Spain he had mingled with kings and queens, associated with noblemen, statesmen, and men of talent. In New York, the merchant was still prince, and the most successful traders, like Astor, were kings enough for themselves and most other people.

Irving took up residence with Ebenezer and his family at 3 Bridge Street. For a few days he went about renewing old friendships. Philadelphia and Baltimore were anxious to tender their own public banquets to the great author. Irving begged off, as later he declined the offer of still another testimonial dinner by the students of Jefferson College (now the University of Virginia) in Charlottesville. Soon he was in Washington conferring with Van Buren, McLane, and President Jackson.

He was a returning diplomat, but the relationship was more than that. America was a smaller country then. The few men of real eminence and accomplishment knew each other and, when they could, tried to be of use to each other. The lines between politician and writer, between artist and scientist, businessman and poet had not yet been sharply drawn.

Fastidious aristocract that he was, Irving yet liked "Old Hickory." He talked to Jackson about his early friend James Paulding who, it was rumored, might lose his navy post. Jackson, surprised, said he had a high opinion of Paulding, so Paulding's job seemed to be safe. Irving tried to repay his debts. Jackson's assurance pleased him. "The more I see of this old cock of the woods, the more I relish his game qualities."

Irving was praised and flattered in Washington. Modest, as he was, and cautious, as he also was, he could not have avoided feeling pleased. Yet he was restless. The old urge to be on the move again assailed him.

Charles Latrobe and Count Pourtales were still in New York. Paulding and Irving took them up the Hudson on a day steamer to show them West Point. Irving renewed his spirit with sight of the beautiful Hudson valley he loved and had written about. It was all new to the Europeans and, as Latrobe said, new to Irving after his seventeen-year absence. Gouverneur Kemble sent his barge to West Point for them and took them to his country place in Highlands, where they spent three hot days. They went on up to the Catskills. It was the first time Irving had actually seen the country he wrote about in "Rip Van Winkle."

The three men decided on a tour of the country farther north. Latrobe and Pourtales found Irving waiting for them, as agreed, in the Tremont Hotel in Boston, and they went from there up into the White Mountains of New Hampshire. They ascended Mount Washington but found the summit shrouded in cloud and mist. In August the three went to Saratoga, then on across New York to Buffalo. They expected to part now, Latrobe and Pourtales traveling into Canada and Irving returning home by way of the Great Lakes and down the Ohio. A chance meeting changed their plans.

The federal government had decided to move frontier Indian tribes from east of the Mississippi into territories west of the river. Aboard a Lake Erie boat, Irving, Latrobe, and Pourtales met Judge Henry Ellsworth of Hartford, Connecticut, one of three commissioners appointed to find suitable lands on which to relocate the tribes. Ellsworth was en route to St. Louis, then to a station at Fort Gibson, about 800 miles up the Arkansas River, and into the wilderness. He invited the three to accompany him.

Curious about the country west of the Alleghenies and the distant prairies, Irving needed little urging. Latrobe and Pourtales forgot about Canada at this promise of new adventure. All three eagerly accepted the new Indian commissioner's invitation. Latrobe expressed the sentiments of them all when he wrote, "It was now—hurra! for the far west!"

chapter X

The Washington Irving who traveled the wild and little-known American West and reported on what he saw, heard, and experienced was not the Washington Irving who made a sentimental pilgrimage to England, dallied in European palaces and drawing rooms, and luxuriated in Queen Elizabeth's apartments in the Alhambra. This was at once an older and a much younger Irving.

He was *the* American man of letters whom England and the United States delighted to honor. He had proved to the world that America could produce a writer and writings of its own that would command the approval of critics as well as appeal to readers everywhere. He was a mature man of international repute.

When he started out to see the far reaches of his own country, Irving was also the boy who had hunted in upper Manhattan with his gun, wandered into Westchester with Paulding, and whose older brother was in the fur trade with the Indians on the New York frontier. He became again the youthful frontiersman who had twice braved the wilderness on journeys to Johnstown and once got as far as Montreal. Irving left Diedrich Knickerbocker and Geoffrey Crayon, Gent. behind when he started west, mounted his horse, and took up his gun again. He had dreamed in Tintern Abbey and the Alhambra, bathed in the dim mists of antiquity. He responded now to the vigor and harsh demands of the raw frontier.

Irving was in good company when he left Ashtabula, Ohio, for Cleveland and then Cincinnati. Pourtales and Latrobe had proved congenial companions crossing the Atlantic and on their expeditions through the northeastern part of the country. Son of a chief justice of the United States, Ellsworth had studied law after graduating from Yale and become mayor of Hartford. He was to become the "Father of the United States Department of Agriculture" as well as the first United States Commissioner of Patents and one of the largest landowners in the middle west.

At Cincinnati September 3, 1832, they boarded a river boat for Louisville. They were delayed at the rapids below Louisville where they found forty or fifty steamers waiting for the water to rise so they could pass through the Portland canal. Then they sailed on down the Ohio and the Mississippi to St. Louis, Missouri, where Irving wrote in his journal: "St. Louis—mixture of French & Indian character—French billiard room—market-place where some are speaking French, some English—put up at the Union Hotel . . . old rackety gambling house—noise of the cue & the billiard ball from morning till night—old French women accosting each other in the street." St. Louis contrasted with Illinois, which, he noted, was famous for children and dogs. He had been in one house with nineteen children and thirty-seven dogs.

At St. Louis, Ellsworth decided to continue on to Fort Gibson by boat, but Latrobe, Pourtales, and Irving obtained a light wagon and horses and outfitted themselves with bearskins and blankets at the American Fur Company's store. It took them a month, stopping at Indian agencies and missions along the way, to reach Fort Gibson, near the junction of the Grand and Arkansas Rivers. Here they learned that a party of rangers, mounted riflemen, had set out three days before to explore the country between the Arkansas and the Red River. They would traverse the Pawnee hunting grounds. Immediately the Irving party decided to catch up with the rangers and, with their protection, enter country still unknown to white men.

The commissioner sent a messenger ahead to instruct the ranger company to wait for them. Then, with a bodyguard of fourteen more rangers, Irving, Ellsworth, Pourtales, and Latrobe set off mounted, with pack horses carrying their equipment. They reached an Osage agency that night.

In his usual fashion, Irving noted quickly everything that impressed him, using the jottings that he later expanded into his full text. In his notebook he wrote, "Creeks—calico hunting shirts—scarlet & blue handkerchief round head—leather & scarlet leggins—groups of riflemen . . . with horses—green blanket coats—half breeds—horses and dogs—hunters in leather shirts—log cabins—stately trees about river, with Virginia creeper."

In *A Tour on the Prairies*, this description of the Creek Indians becomes,

> They dress in calico hunting-shirts, of various brilliant colors, decorated with bright fringes, and belted with broad girdles, embroidered with beads; they have leggins of dressed deer-skins, or of green or scarlet cloth, with embroidered knee-bands and tassels; their moccasins are fancifully wrought and ornamented, and they wear gaudy handkerchiefs tastefully bound round their heads.

In his notes Irving simply mentioned the horses and dogs around the Osage agency. He brings the animals alive in his book with this description of a blacksmith shoeing a horse.

> An old trapper, in leathern hunting-frock and moccasins, had placed his rifle against a work-bench, while he superintended the operation and gossiped about his hunting exploits; several large dogs were lounging in and out of the shop, or sleeping in the sunshine, while a little cur, with head cocked on one side, and one ear erect, was watching, with that curiosity common to little dogs, the process of shoeing the horse, as if studying the art, or waiting for his turn to be shod.

Pourtales and Latrobe had already hired an Osage and French half-breed named Antoine as servant and handyman. A voluble, boastful, ridiculous little man, "Tonish" becomes a figure of fun throughout the expedition. Ellsworth and Irving, who now traveled together, hired another half-breed of very different sort. Pierre Beatte was cold and laconic, sullen and saturnine. An experienced trapper and woodsman, he took small pains to hide his contempt for both his employers and the rangers. Irving describes with admiration not so much the man as the frontier type.

> He came mounted on one horse and leading another, which seemed to be well packed with supplies for the expedition. Beatte was evidently an "old soldier," as to the art of taking care of himself and looking out for emergencies. Finding that he was in government employ, being engaged by the Commissioner, he had drawn rations of flour and bacon, and put them up so as to be weather-proof. In addition to the horse for the road and for ordinary service, which was a rough, hardy animal, he had another for hunting. This was of a mixed breed like himself, being a cross of the domestic stock with the wild horse of the prairies . . . He had taken care to have his horses well shod at the Agency. He came prepared at all points for war or hunting: his rifle on his shoulder, his powder-horn and bullet-pouch at his side, his hunting-knife stuck in his belt, and coils of cordage at his saddle-bow, which we were told were lariats, or noosed cords, used in catching wild horse.
>
> Thus equipped and provided, an Indian hunter

> on a prairie is like a cruiser on the ocean, perfectly independent of the world, and competent to self-protection and self-maintenance.

Irving noted the nondescript horde of trappers, half-breeds, and Indians around the agency; the tall Osage, bare-breasted, blankets wrapped around their waists. They were handsome and dignified in contrast to the gaudy Creeks. The rangers lounged during a morning break, some shooting at marks, others half-asleep in beds of foliage, others gossiping. He liked the Robin Hood appearance of the camps as they pushed on, and was awed by vistas of the endless prairie. He was amused by the lying bravado of Tonish, with his Indian wife and brood of children. He admired the noble savage, the noble wild horse, and a faithful blind dog they came upon silently tracing his lost master through the woods.

Irving found the great grasslands where there was no sign of human existence far lonelier than the deep forest. He felt indignation at the brutal treatment of the Indian by the white man. In his journal he noted an incident. "Just then we meet old lantern jawed man who had lost his horse—had just met with Osage leading him back, who said he had wandered to their camp. Lantern jawed man was for tying him up & giving him a swing of rushes, but we interfered."

Irving is much more severe in his full account of the incident in "A Tour on the Prairies." The red-haired squatter, rifle in hand, caught up with the expedition and rode along with them threatening to kill the Indian thief. He was busily swearing vengeance when they met an Osage boy on his way to return the strayed horse.

> I was struck with his appearance. He was about nineteen or twenty years of age, but well grown, with the fine Roman countenance common to his tribe; and as he rode, with his blanket wrapped round his loins, his naked bust would have furnished a model for a statuary. He was mounted on a beautiful piebald horse, a mottled white and brown, of the wild breed of the prairies, decorated with a broad collar, from which hung in front a tuft of horse-hair dyed of a bright scarlet.

The squatter was enraged when Irving and his companions refused to let him tie up and lash the boy who was returning his property. Irving despised him.

> Such . . . is too often the administration of law on the frontier, "Lynch's law," as it is technically termed, in which the plaintiff is apt to be witness, jury, judge, and executioner, and the defendant to be convicted and punished on mere presumption; and in this way, I am convinced, are occasioned many of those heart-burnings and resentments among the Indians, which lead to retaliation, and end in Indian wars. When I compared the open, noble countenance and frank demeanor of the young Osage with the sinister visage and high-handed conduct of the frontiersman, I felt little doubt on whose back a lash would be most meritoriously bestowed.

Washington Irving did more than watch and record on this expedition into the Pawnee hunting grounds. He took an active part in all that was going on. The dreaming antiquarian of Bracebridge Hall who had been a guest in Scott's Abbotsford soon gave up his tent and, like the others, slept on a bearskin spread at the foot of a tree with his saddlebags for pillow. He never slept more soundly.

Irving learned the dependence of the plainsman on his horse when he lamed his mount in leaping a brook. Too generous to reclaim another good horse which he had allowed Tonish, he rode an indifferent pony for a time. All of the rangers were continually swapping horses, guns, and knives. Irving joined in. Through judicious trading he acquired a full-blooded sorrel, the best horse in the troop. He said he felt like another being with this spirited animal under him. Within a few days the sorrel was following him about like a dog asking to be petted. If Irving sat reading when they made camp, the horse would poke his nose between man and book.

Irving was as admiring as all the others when Pierre Beatte chased, caught, and tamed, a magnificent wild horse. He thrilled to the buffalo hunt and acquitted himself like an experienced plainsman. As the herd thundered over the prairie, Irving raced his eager horse alongside a huge beast, trying to get within pistol range. Twice his horse got frightened at the evil appearance of the shaggy buffalo at close quarters and shied off. On the third attempt, Irving managed to race him close enough to discharge both pistols at his prey. Both misfired. Their locks were worn, and the priming had shaken out in the headlong gallop.

He reloaded his uncertain weapons and in a new dash tried again. Again his pistols misfired. Latrobe had brought down a buffalo with his shotgun. Irving borrowed the gun, galloped after the herd, chose an animal, and brought it down with one shot. Excited and flushed with triumph, Irving raced up to the fallen buffalo. His elation evaporated when he found it dying slowly and agonizingly. He primed his pistols and remorsefully shot it through the heart.

Most of the rangers were young, excited by their first wilderness trial, and impatient of discipline. When game abounded, they brought down buffalo and venison with abandon, cut out the choice parts, discarded the rest. They refused to consider the morrow. They would jerk no meat, make no provision for the next day. American vandalism is an old habit from these days of frontier plenty. Irving sometimes lingered when the Ellsworth expedition broke camp in the morning. It was always a shambles of felled and partly hewn trees, smoldering fires, great chunks of venison and buffalo meat still on the spits on which they had been roasted and hacked at by the knives of the men. Hides, horns, wild turkeys killed but not even plucked, uncooked haunches of venison lay about. The turkey buzzards circled overhead waiting for Irving to go.

They met Delawares, Creeks, Osage, Pawnees. Irving describes one encounter with a foraging party of Indians.

> The worthy Commissioner now remembered his mission as a pacificator, and made a speech exhorting them to abstain from all offensive acts against the Pawnees; informing them of the plan of their father at Washington, to put an end to all war among his red children; and assuring them that he was sent to the frontier to establish a universal peace. . . .
>
> The Indians listened to the speech with their customary silence and decorum; after which, exchanging a few words among themselves, they bade us

> farewell, and pursued their way across the prairie.
>
> Fancying that I saw a lurking smile in the countenance of our interpreter, Beatte, I privately inquired what the Indians had said to each other after hearing the speech. The leader, he said, had observed to his companions, that, as their great father intended so soon to put an end to all warfare, it behooved them to make the most of the little time that was left them. So they had departed, with redoubled zeal, to pursue their project of horse-stealing!

Irving exploded the myth of the strong, silent Indian. Their habit was to keep quiet before white men, then mock them when they were by themselves. The Indians saw everything at a glance but reserved comment until they were alone. They were great mimics, clowns, and talkers, boasting of their exploits and gossiping as earnestly as any other breed of men. "As far as I can judge," Irving decided, "the Indian of poetical fiction is, like the shepherd of pastoral romance, a mere personification of imaginary attributes."

Three of the rangers came down with measles and had to be left behind. It surprised Irving to discover that the Indians and many of the rugged outdoorsmen, like Pierre Beatte, were badly crippled by rheumatism. Continual exposure to the elements took its toll.

He crossed a river in what he called a cockleshell bark of buffalo hide, and he delighted in the days and nights. "It was a splendid autumnal evening. The horizon, after sunset, was of a clear apple-green, rising into a delicate lake which gradually lost itself in a deep purple blue.

One narrow streak of cloud, of a mahogany color, edged with amber and gold, floated in the west, and just beneath it was the evening star, shining with the pure brilliancy of a diamond." A concert of insects soothed Irving as he watched the sky.

Before long the rangers and the whole party were paying for their heedless extravagance. They rode out of game country. They had no bread, no salt. Worse, they had no coffee, which the Indians as well as the frontiersmen drank all through this country. The hunters of the party flushed a few turkeys, but these were insufficient. Soon they were completely out of food of any kind, and the days and nights were getting colder. Irving awoke one morning to find his blankets covered with hoarfrost, though, he admitted, he had slept warmly and well.

Urged on by gaunt hunger, the expedition was struggling back to the Osage agency from which it had set out: "push on, horses fagged—arrive at log house owned by white man with black, fat wife—delightful sight of hogs—poultry, crowing of cocks &c.—horse pricks his ears—Stop at the door—Cap [captain of the ranger troop] & officer eating at a table—huge iron pot with beef & turnips—put in for a share, fat negress gives a plate heaping with beef & turnips, corn bread & butter—apologises for giving it in such poor style!"

Ellsworth and Irving, Latrobe and Pourtales spent the night at the agency, then set out for Fort Gibson, where they arrived tattered, weatherbeaten, and travel-stained, "but in high health and spirits."

Two days later, Irving left Fort Gibson by river steamer. His companions were sorry to see him go. Latrobe has described him as good-natured and humorous throughout all of their journey into the wilderness. Irving continued to note his impressions as he sailed on down to New Orleans, whence he returned to New York. Distinctions between the various Indian tribes interested him particularly.

> Choctaws—much attached to the whites—boast that they have never killed a white man . . . Chickasaws—amalgamated with the Choctaws—their language nearly the same—their women handsome . . . The Quipaws a small remnant of a tribe below Little Rock . . . The bravest and finest race is the Delawares . . . all their equipments of the best—their camp kettles of brass . . . Pawnees—when they attack in the prairies it is necessary—to tie your horses head to head in a circle. They come round you with feathers, mantles, &c., fluttering—great whoops & yells that strike panic into the horses . . . keep in the Prairies—will not follow into the thickets.

It is customary to find Irving's books about the American West inferior to his earlier books. Irving himself is partly responsible for this. Often self-deprecating, he is almost querulous in the introduction to *A Tour on the Prairies,* which was published in 1835. He said he had felt pressed and harassed by the demands made upon him for the speedy production of an American book. He had been traveling for his own pleasure, but the newspapers had reported that he was seeking new material. They had advertised his new book as being on press even before he had begun to write it.

What he had to say, Irving said, was not new. Others

had written well on the same subject. His book was merely "a simple narrative of every-day occurrences, such as happen to every one who travels the prairies. I have no wonders to describe . . ."

People dismiss a man's pretentions as boasting. Usually they are eager to accept his stated low opinion of his work. They made a mistake in accepting Irving's here. *A Tour on the Prairies* is not "Rip Van Winkle" or the *Alhambra*. Irving did not intend it to be. He was handling actual not nostalgically romantic material, and his object was not reverie and whimsy but graphic reporting. Irving is always accurate and acute. His quiet, easily flowing style often hides the sharpness, but his narrative in *A Tour on the Prairies* is firm and often exciting. The book is packed with his observations on places and people. The pace is leisurely, but the story is vivid.

The city-bred New Yorker who had hobnobbed with the famous and powerful over half of Europe and achieved recognition on two continents for unique and lasting achievement was not as much at home on the prairies as Tonish or Beatte. For years he had been accustomed to the polished society of a far older and more settled civilization than that of even the cities of the eastern United States. He was much older than Pourtales, considerably older than Latrobe, eight years older than Ellsworth. Irving found some of the uncouthness of the West disturbing, but he was resilient and proved himself adaptable. He endured the hardships of the expedition along with the most rugged of his companions. He rode hard, slept hard, ate hard, hunted and feasted, or, when food gave out, went without as the others did. He may have thought

—or said—that he had little to say in *A Tour on the Prairies*, but for more than 130 years other writers have been making good use, sometimes unacknowledged, of what Irving experienced and recorded in the West.

This same year Charles Latrobe dedicated the two volumes of his book, *The Rambler in North America*, to "Washington Irving, Esq. in Token of Affectionate Esteem and Remembrance."

Undoubtedly Irving was pleased. He was also hard at work on new projects of several kinds.

chapter XI

Washington Irving knew at first hand what he wrote of in *A Tour on the Prairies.* His two other books on the American West were not reports of his own experiences. They were based on records, documents, journals, and diaries kept by venturesome travelers; on his reading; and on conversations with adventurers.

Irving liked the frontier, the plains and the mountains, the Indians, the wild life. He admired the tough frontiersmen. Like Sir Walter Scott who had been drawn to the Scottish Border country and Henry Thoreau who loved the Massachusetts woods and would have been an Indian had he been able, Irving had responded to the appeal of stream and forest for as long as he could remember.

John Jacob Astor, son of a German butcher, had landed in America the year after Irving's birth with $25 and a stock of seven flutes to set himself up in business. He worked for a short time as a baker's apprentice, then got a job in a fur store at $2 a week. On his way across the Atlantic he had met another German, who had been in the fur trade with the Indians, thus Astor knew what he wanted. His marriage brought him $300 in cash and a wife who knew furs. Astor went into business for himself.

He worked hard. He bought cheap and sold dear. He took risks. He traded in furs with the North West Company in Montreal. He traveled the frontier posts himself to buy directly from the Indians, then shipped his pelts abroad. By 1800, John Jacob Astor virtually controlled the fur trade in the United States.

His ships were sailing to Europe and the Orient. He had wealth and political as well as commercial power. What he wanted was more. In fact, he wanted it all. Astor decided to drive French and Canadian interests out of the country and to establish a monopoly in furs. In 1808 he founded the American Fur Company—he was the company. He got concessions through his influence in Washington and embarked on a heroic venture.

Astor decided to set up a principal fur post at the mouth of the Columbia River in Oregon. His outposts throughout all of the country west of the Rocky Mountains would do the trapping and the buying from the Indians, then send the pelts to the station and factory on the Pacific coast. There they would be picked up by Astor's ships and ferried to New York, London, or China, then the world's richest markets for furs. The ships would bring back cargoes of oriental goods for sale on the American east coast or in Europe. In addition, by arrangement with Saint Petersburg, Astor planned to become the sole supplier of Russian America which, with its capital at Sitka, controlled the fur trade in what is now Alaska.

It was an ambitious and daring undertaking. Thomas Jefferson's secretary, Meriwether Lewis, and William Clark of Virginia and Kentucky had concluded their great exploration into the Northwest only two years before. That expedition had been the first to travel from the Missouri over the unknown Rockies down the Columbia through Oregon to the Pacific. Though the stirring success of their exploration had been reported to Congress in 1806, the details were still unknown to the public when Astor made his plans. They were not to be published until 1814. Astor was pushing into thousands of miles of virgin wilderness and unknown territory when he plotted his strategy in 1808.

Washington Irving was fascinated when he heard the story from Astor in a long talk soon after his return to New York. He had dined with the fur lords in Montreal, talked with their factors and trappers. He had lived with Henry Brevoort. He was fresh from his own western experiences. His imagination was fired as Astor talked. It was an epic tale.

Astor, too, was insistent that he write it, and, as Irving wrote his nephew, Pierre Munro Irving, enlisting his research help, Astor was "a strong-minded man." Astor turned all his records, all the letters, all the journals kept by his various men over to Irving. Working at Hell Gate or in Astor's townhouse in New York, Pierre waded through them. He chose the most important for his uncle's perusal and use. Irving drew on these papers, on his own experience, on the full reports of Lewis and Clark and on the accounts of other western explorers. From all of these he wrote *Astoria.*

Astoria is a formidable book. It is a volume of nearly 700 pages in the Kinderhook Edition of the works of Washington Irving, almost three times as long as *A Tour on the Prairies* in the same edition. It is an exciting book charged with the spirit of great adventure, vibrant with conflict, and somber with tragedy. It is a book alive with incident and anecdote, redolent of wind and weather. Dark forest, impassable mountains, raging rivers are more than background. They are characters as real as the Canadian *voyageurs and coureurs de bois,* Kentucky riflemen, and a score of Indian tribes. Astor lives in its pages. So do his gentlemanly and ungentlemanly agents, the indestructible trappers, the noble and ignoble savages, and Washington Irving.

Astoria has been disparaged—mostly by those who, blithely applying late twentieth-century economic morality to early nineteenth-century circumstances, can never have taken the trouble to read it. These critics condemn it as a sort of public relations book written for an economic imperialist and probably paid for by Astor. It is not such a book, and Astor did not pay Irving to write it. He paid Pierre Munro Irving $3,000 for his research, but the nephew emphatically denied rumors which sprang up that Astor also paid Washington Irving. Though he knew him from his youth to Astor's death, Irving was always careful not to become financially indebted to the powerful older man. "He was too proverbially a rich man," Irving said, "for me to permit the shadow of a pecuniary favor to rest on our intercourse."

Astor had set out to attain his ambitious objective of founding the station which became Astoria only after long and careful planning. He met in Washington with government officials and with the Russian minister, even sent an emissary directly to Saint Petersburg. Then, hiring men away from his chief competitor, the North West Company in Canada, he divided his forces. One party he sent by sea from New York around Cape Horn and up the California coast to Oregon. The other party, headed by his chief agent, Wilson B. Hunt, he sent overland from Mackinac, where lakes Huron and Michigan meet, to the mouth of the Columbia.

Irving begins at the beginning in *Astoria* with the preparation for the founding of the capital of Astor's envisioned fur empire. Then he follows the fortunes of the *Tonquin* and the men who sailed in her from New York; then the trails of the men who fought their way west from Mackinac.

Astor's was no mean or merely commercial undertaking, nor was it so regarded at the time. President Jefferson, who encouraged Astor in the venture, said, "I considered, as a great public acquisition, the commencement of a settlement on that point of the western coast of America, and looked forward with gratification to the time when its descendants would spread themselves through the whole length of the coast, covering it with free and independent Americans unconnected with us but by the ties of blood and interest, and enjoying like us the rights of self-government."

Four Astor partners, twelve clerks, thirteen Canadian *voyageurs*, canoemen who had enlisted for five-year terms, and a group of artisans embarked from New York in the *Tonquin*. Under command of Jonathan Thorne, a naval lieutenant on leave, the ship, which had a crew of twenty, carried a cargo of trade goods, seed, and the frame of a schooner to be built in Oregon for use in coastal trade. The *Tonquin* mounted ten guns.

It was an odd voyage that began September 10, 1810, and lasted many months. Thorne was a strict disciplinarian and something of a martinet. The *voyageurs* were unruly and incorrigible; and his other passengers were not having any restrictions placed on their behavior either. The captain and his fur-trade company were continually at odds. There were quarrels and disrupting incidents aboard and at stops in the South Seas, but in April 1811 the *Tonquin* finally reached her destination at what became Astoria.

The Chinook Indians swarmed around the invaders. They were used to having white men arrive in ships and had had their sharp wits made sharper in trade with the fur-seeking vessels that plied the Pacific coast. The Indians were there, and so was the competition. Through the treachery of a subordinate, the North West Company had learned of Astor's plans and had already established men in outposts not far away.

Immediately the Astorians went about building their fort and factory, but under severe difficulties. Though Astor, who had learned his lessons on the frontier years before, had warned against it, his men allowed Indians aboard ship. There Captain Thorne got into a dispute with a chief named Nookamis. The chief had been trading craftily with less resolute skippers for years. This time his cunning led to Thorne's kicking Nookamis and his pelts off the ship.

The enraged Indians returned the next day with twenty secretly armed allies. A desperate hand-to-hand battle ensued on the deck of the *Tonquin.* Thorne was killed almost immediately. One of the other Americans was felled by a war club, tossed overboard, and knifed to death by the Indian women waiting in the canoes. The ship's clerk, Lewis, was stabbed in the back but managed to crawl to the cabin over the debris of dead and wounded. With four others he turned a murderous fire on the Chinooks. They fled, and Lewis sent the four ashore under cover of darkness. He remained alone in the cabin.

Unmanned, the *Tonquin* tossed, helpless, on the sea. The next morning, Lewis appeared on deck and waved the waiting Indians aboard. They raced to plunder. Lewis, who had disappeared below deck, waited until enough of them were aboard, then fired the ship's powder magazine, blowing up the ship, himself, and about one hundred Chinooks.

No mellifluous style here, no dreaming poesy, but harsh fact vividly reported. Irving tells this story with force and vigor.

Intent on vengeance, crowds of hostile Indians threatened the handful of men left at Astoria. One of the partners, M'Dougal, kept them at bay, then cowed them by a ruse. Grasping a small bottle, he threatened to pull its cork and loose the smallpox among them. The Indians, who had seen white man's diseases decimate more than one tribe, were too frightened to attack.

The Astorians went on with their building of the post. They assembled the schooner they had brought with them, christened her the *Dolly,* and launched the first American vessel built on the Oregon coast.

Meanwhile, Wilson Hunt's party of some sixty men was having its troubles too. Despite hindrances from competing fur companies in St. Louis, they got under way, but difficulties mounted as they began boating up the Missouri. At Charette they met Daniel Boone, now a tall, erect old man of almost ninety, who had just returned from the wilderness with sixty beaver skins. They came upon few other friendly people. They met Osage and Sioux. They made hard portages, killed game, smoked peace pipes with some Indians, skirmished with others. They horse-traded with the Arickaras, traded with the "free-booting Crows," as Irving usually calls them, and with the Cheyenne.

Like the rangers with whom Irving rode the prairies, the trappers, interpreters, *voyageurs,* and riflemen of Hunt's expedition lived well when game was plentiful. Like them, they suffered when no game was to be had. Famine overtook the party as winter set in. They ate dogs. When they could trade for one with the Indians, they feasted on horse flesh. One starving French-Canadian trapper became so overjoyed at the promise of such food that when he was signaled from shore he jumped up and down in his canoe, was swept overboard, and drowned.

After severe hardships of many kinds, Hunt's party eventually reached the Columbia, followed its valley to the coast, and arrived at Astoria.

Both arms of the Astor expedition had now reached their destination and the comparative safety of their newly-built fort, but they had come not only to establish the post, but also to supply it with furs. Men sent to set up outposts fared badly. Indians ambushed them, stole their food, their horses, even their rifles. On one occasion they stripped their victims naked and rode off leaving them to the wilderness. Indian law was an eye for an eye, blood for blood. They avenged themselves for any slight, real or fancied, by a white man on the next white man who fell into their eager clutches.

Men from Astoria came upon a small party which had left the Wilson expedition on its way out to hunt and trap on their own. They had been set upon and robbed by the Arapahays. The Indians had left them their guns, but there had been no game where they were, and they could not catch fish enough in the streams. Somehow they had managed to survive the winter, but they were starving when they were found.

According to the survivors, one of their number had villainously deserted them. Irving suspected that the truth was far more gruesome. "Certain dark doubts and surmises were afterward circulated concerning the fate of that poor fellow, which, if true, showed to what a desperate state of famine his comrades had been reduced."

Irving is more outspoken about cannibalism in describing an incident which occurred when another party of Astor trappers was forced to go for days without food. Wild with hunger, one of the French Canadians approached the leader with a suggestion. They could go no farther without food. It was better that one should die than that they all should perish. He proposed that they cast lots to see who should be sacrificed to their hunger. Not until the leader threatened to shoot him if he persisted did the man change his mind. A day later the party managed to kill an old buffalo. The ravenous men devoured part of the animal raw.

A brutal incident did not improve relations between the American Fur Company men and the Indians. The Indians were persistent thieves. The Crow and Sioux were piratical, violent in their burglaries. Others were sly pilferers.

One of the Astor leaders named Clarke was a tall, stately gentleman of some dignity who tried to carry his civilized habits into the wilderness. He preferred to drink from a silver goblet given him by Astor. After quaffing from it "with a magnificent air" he then locked it in a case which he kept in his tent. One night he forgot to lock the case. A Nez Percé Indian slipped into camp, stole the goblet and other booty, and slipped out.

When the thief was caught, Clarke sentenced him to death. The Indians begged for the man's life. Other Astorians argued against the execution. Clarke, who hated Indians and held their lives as cheaply as those of the wild animals they trapped, was unmoved. He had a gibbet built of oars, hauled the trussed-up Nez Percé screaming to the gallows, and hanged him. As Clarke's companions had feared, the Indians avenged themselves at the first opportunity.

The War of 1812 put a sharp end to Astor's heroic venture. Astoria might well have succeeded, and Irving believed it could have been saved. He blames M'Dougal for disloyally selling out cheaply to waiting agents of the North West Company of Canada and the government of the United States for letting Astoria go to England almost by default.

The Indians themselves wanted to help the Americans defend Astoria against the British. Albert Gallatin, who was bitterly opposed to the war, backed Astor's request for military aid, but President Monroe was not "disposed in all probability to commit himself by any direct countenance or overt act." With the North West Company in triumphant possession of all its furs, equipment, and outposts, Astoria reluctantly surrendered to the enemy.

A British sloop sailed into harbor, and its captain—incensed when he found that the North West Company had hauled off the loot he expected to gain—took over. "Captain Black, attended by his officers, entered the fort, caused the British standard to be erected, broke a bottle of wine, and declared, in a loud voice, that he took possession of the establishment and of the country in the name of his Britannic Majesty, changing the name of Astoria to that of Fort George."

There is no mistaking Irving's patriotic indignation. His mother had been English, his father a Scot. Irving himself had lived in England and loved the country, its past and its people, but he was as thoroughly American in sympathy as the man to whom he owed his given name. He had served briefly in this very War of 1812 with high military rank if no very military duties.

While he was working on *Astoria*, Irving talked to everyone he could who knew the Far West so that he could enliven the written records at his disposal with the oral reports of men who had experienced the wilderness. At John Jacob Astor's Hell Gate estate he met Captain Benjamin Louis Eulalie de Bonneville of the United States Army.

He was quickly attracted to the West Pointer of French descent who had served at a number of frontier posts, became interested in the Indians and trappers, and decided to lead an expedition into the Rocky Mountains. He obtained a two-year leave of absence and army approval of his plans. In New York, some of it evidently from Astor, he wangled financial backing. With a strong force of men he disappeared into the fastnesses of the western mountains.

No word came back for so long that they were given up for dead. His leave having expired, Bonneville's name was stricken from army records. When Irving met him in 1835, he had just returned, very much alive, from more than three years in the western wilds.

Undoubtedly, Bonneville had been as much attracted by the profits which he saw could be made in the fur trade as by any scientific or patriotic motive. His purpose was gain, but Irving saw him as a daring adventurer, a simple-hearted soldier with a nice taste for Shakespeare, Corneille, and Voltaire, and all the courage Irving so admired in the pioneers of the fur trade.

He came upon Bonneville again in Washington where the bald-headed officer was trying to get himself reinstated in the army (Bonneville served gallantly in the Mexican War and was made a brigadier general in 1865) and to put his expedition notes and papers into intelligible form. He was making hard work of it. Irving could not resist the opportunity for one more go at his western writing. Bonneville turned the mass of papers over to him to shape into a book, and Irving went to work. In 1837 he published *The Adventures of Captain Bonneville, U.S.A. in the Rocky Mountains of the Far West*, "Digested from his journal, and illustrated from various other sources."

Like Irving's two other books about the West, *Bonneville* is a vigorous account of Indians and wild animals, of bitter hardships, and of riotous celebrations. Again, in his imagination, Washington Irving, depending on his horse for transport and his rifle for food, toiled up mountains, shot rapids, fought off attacking Indians, and regained civilization laden with choice pelts.

This book resembles the other two, but this time Irving's hero and his band get into new and different territory. Like Lewis and Clark, Astor's men had traversed French and Indian lands. The Bonneville expedition got into Spanish California as well.

Washington Irving was prophetic about California. After talking of San Diego, Santa Barbara, Monterey, the Bay of San Francisco, and Bondago—which the Russians had taken and fortified—Irving had this to say: "The Russians have always a ship of war upon this station . . . Recent surveys have likewise been made, both by the Russians and the English, and we have little doubt, that, at no very distant day, this neglected, and, until recently, almost unknown region, will be found to possess sources of wealth sufficient to sustain a powerful and prosperous empire."

Irving did not know that California would become part of the United States. He could not foresee the gold rush of 1849. He could hardly have envisioned present-day Los Angeles and San Francisco. He certainly could never have imagined Hollywood and the degree to which entertainers and electronic entertainment would dominate American life, but in 1837 Washington Irving foresaw something of the possibilities in California's future.

As Robert Louis Stevenson did almost a half century later, Irving commented wonderingly on the dashing horsemanship of the Mexicans in California. They spent the greater part of their lives in the saddle, and their feats astonished Bonneville and his men. Irving described a Mexican dragoon who reminded him of the caballeros of Andalusian Spain.

> A Mexican dragoon . . . is represented as arrayed in a round blue jacket, with red cuffs and collar; blue velvet breeches, unbuttoned at the knees to show his white stockings; bottinas of deer-skin; a round-crowned Andalusian hat, and his hair cued. On the pommel of his saddle, he carries balanced a long musket, with fox-skin round the lock. He is cased in a cuirass of double-fold deer-skin, and carries a bull's hide shield; he is forked in a Moorish saddle, high before and behind; his feet are thrust into wooden box stirrups, of Moorish fashion, and a tremendous pair of iron spurs, fastened by chains, jingle at his heels. Thus equipped, and suitably mounted, he considers himself the glory of California, and the terror of the universe.

Irving admired other characteristics of the Californians less than he did their horsemanship. He particularly detested some of their sports. A favorite with the wheeling and cavorting horseman who galloped about twirling their lariats was the bullfight. Irving had become an enthusiast in Spain and he had no quarrel with the Mexicans who swarmed to contests of man and horse against bull. But he detested the fights, which the Mexicans enjoyed, between a wild bull and a bear. The cruelty of this was not to Irving's taste. Even less to his taste was another California pastime.

In California as elsewhere the Indians were given to horse-stealing. Warfare between the adept marauders and their bereft victims was continuous. Two Mexican trappers who joined the Bonneville party proved themselves especially skillful at a sport which developed out of this conflict.

Viewing all Indians as enemies, they vied with each other in tormenting and killing them. Bonneville's force had murdered Indians enough, often without cause, on the way to California, but this was different. When the expedition got into country frequented by the poor Root Digger Indians, the two Mexicans put on a brilliant display of their skill. They gave the Root Diggers no chance. ". . . the Mexicans, very probably, charged them with the sin of horse-stealing; we have no other mode of accounting for the infamous barbarities of which, according to their own story, they were guilty; hunting the poor Indians like wild beasts, and killing them without mercy. The Mexicans excelled at this savage sport; chasing their unfortunate victims at full speed; noosing them round the neck with their lassos, and then dragging them to death!"

Some of his men may have been entertained, but Bonneville felt only horror and disgust. Irving's comment is, "Had he exerted a little of the Lynch law of the wilderness, and hanged those dexterous horsemen in their own lassos, it would but have been a well-merited and salutary act of retributive justice."

All of *Bonneville* is not as unpleasant. There were lighter incidents.

At one point the captain and a party of twenty-three of his more than one hundred men returned in summer to the Columbia River where they met another party in the service of the Hudson's Bay Company. As Hudson's Bay men had several times befriended them, Bonneville invited the leader and his officers to a hunter's banquet at his camp.

There was plenty to eat but little to drink. As his chief guest was depressed over some recent misfortunes, Bonneville particularly regretted that he had no wine to raise his spirits. Then he had an idea. With him he had a half-filled keg of honey. He filled the rest of the keg with alcohol and stirred the "fiery and mellifluous ingredients."

It was mead of a kind, and it worked merrily. The Canadian guest drank deep and often. He became voluble. He sang loudly until he fell asleep. When he awoke, he went at the honey and alcohol again. "The morning found him still upon the field of action, but in sad and sorrowful condition . . ."

Bonneville's expedition was a financial failure, but the information he brought back was of value. He was fortunate in having Washington Irving for reporter. He regained his captaincy and moved ahead in his army career. His first assignment after reinstatement was to the same Fort Gibson from which Irving had set out with Ellsworth and Latrobe in 1832. Bonneville Salt Flats in Utah was named in his honor, and the great hydroelectric dam on the Columbia, some forty miles east of Portland, bears his name.

Irving's three books about the early American West do not match *The Sketch Book* or *The Alhambra* in charm and reflective grace. They have not the whimsy of his Knickerbocker history or the scholarship of his *Columbus* and *Granada*. What "A Tour on the Prairies," *Astoria*, and *The Adventures of Captain Bonneville, U.S.A.* do have is vigor and vividness.

Irving's always smooth and sometimes placid style disguises some of the starkness of the adventures he describes. His pleasantness seems almost to soothe away torments and cruelties, starvation, madness, murder; but they are there. Because he was Irving, in love with the romantic past, the friend and admirer of Sir Walter Scott, he saw romance in the plains and wilderness, as he saw romance everywhere he looked; but reality is in these stories too. Under his hand, they became adventures, and his adventurers became heroes, but it was original and authentic history that Irving wrote. He reported the actual, and in so doing interpreted some of his country to itself.

Irving valued the wilderness, the Indian, the wild animals, the rugged trappers and frontiersmen. He spoke out for all of them. There were many Indians and many buffalo still to be slaughtered when Irving wrote, and they were duly slaughtered, but not with his approval.

The hunters, trappers, Indians, and frontiersmen have disappeared as the American frontier has disappeared, but Americans have not let them go willingly. They live on in the paintings of Frederic Remington, Charles Russell, George Catlin, Peter Rindisbacher, and a dozen other artists. They are dramatized in motion pictures and on television because men still cherish the primitive poetry and even the violence, the simpler conflicts of frontier days, and look upon them with the same feelings of romantic nostalgia with which Irving viewed England and Spain.

Irving knew as he wrote that much of the life he had seen and experienced or learned of from others was doomed to disappear. He would have kept some of what seemed good in it to him. He wished that the Indian names for the rivers and mountains which Wilson Hunt and his men crossed or climbed could be retained. "As the aboriginal names of these magnificent regions are yet in existence, the Indian names might easily be recovered, which, besides being in general more sonorous and musical, would remain mementoes of the primitive lords of the soil, of whom in a little while scarce any trace will be left."

A few had written of the West before Irving. Countless stories have been written about it since, with Irving's work for accurate source of what it was like in the early years of the nineteenth century. He did more than leave a record. He struck a chord to which Americans still respond. Despite atom bombs and some of the other amenities of twentieth-century internationalism, this is still a new country, a country wrested from the wilderness not too long ago, a country which had had a brawling frontier for most of its existence.

The chord that Irving struck can still be heard throughout his American books and even in the brief jottings in his journal.

> Camp—fire—meat roasted on sticks—savory—our salon of trees lighted up by fire—sky & stars in centre—bat flitting across—faces of men & black boy roasting meat—greyhound with spectral face—we sit on bear skins & the meat put on spits before us—cut it off with knife & eat—coffee . . .

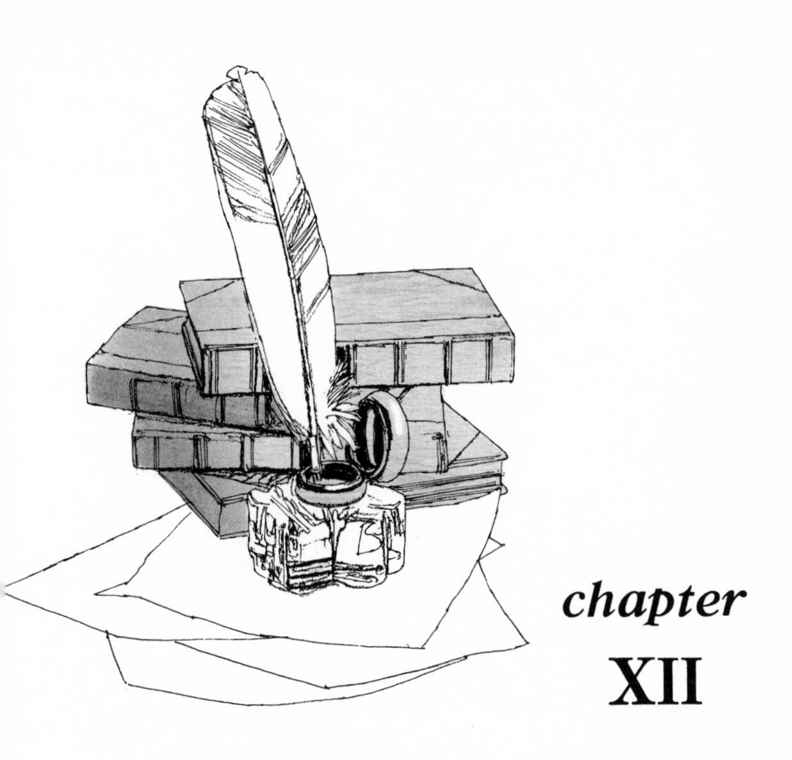

chapter XII

In *The Alhambra,* Irving described himself as a haphazard loiterer about the world who was prone to linger in its pleasant places. Irving continued to wander after his return to his native country—he always would—but he was too concerned with reality to have much time for dreaming.

He wrote a good deal of *Astoria* at Astor's Hell Gate estate, working rapidly in the country quiet and in the pleasant society of Astor, Pierre, and the poet Fitz-Greene Halleck, who was Astor's well-paid secretary. It was a pleasant and convenient arrangement, for it gave Irving living and working surroundings that were rather more than comfortable while he was waiting for his own new home to be ready for occupancy.

In April 1835, Irving bought ten acres of land and a little, old Dutch stone house just south of Tarrytown on the Hudson. This was in the heart of the Sleepy Hollow Country he had made famous in *The Sketch Book.* In that book he had written, "If ever I should wish for a retreat, whither I might steal from the world and its distractions, and dream quietly away the remnant of a troubled life, I know of none more promising than this little valley."

The house, on a high wooded bank facing that part of the wide Hudson known as Tappan Zee, was that which he had fancifully made the paternal home of Katrina Van Tassel in "The Legend of Sleepy Hollow." In *Wolfert's Roost* he described it as "a little, old-fashioned stone mansion, all made up of gable ends, and as full of angles and corners as an old cocked hat."

Irving might have kept the name "Wolfert's Rust," meaning "Wolfert's Rest" or, as it became in its corrupted form, "Wolfert's Roost." He might have called it Abbotsford or Alhambra after places he loved. With as good a reason, he might have dubbed it Shadyside or Riverview. His choice, as indicative of his taste and temperament as of house and site, was Sunnyside.

He hired carpenters and masons and began at once to build a substantial stone house about the remains of the older place which was well over a hundred years old. At first he intended Sunnyside to be only a rural retreat for himself and a place where Ebenezer and his daughters could vacation in summer. Irving designed his home, planned for the space he thought he would need, then, like most home-builders, found the construction more time-consuming, extensive, and expensive than he had counted on.

For most of his life Irving had lived out of trunks and traveling bags. Unmarried, he had had no fixed abode. He wanted a home of his own amid pleasant and congenial surroundings, not too far from the homes of his friends like Paulding, Kemble, Brevoort, and others, all of whom had places up or down the river.

A Tour on the Prairies, published by Carey, Lea and Blanchard in Philadelphia, brought him a good price. Murray, to whose publishing house he had returned, brought out an edition in London. When *Astoria* was ready for the press, Irving got $4,000 for it from his Philadelphia publishers and another $2,500 or so from the London edition. The money was coming in, but it was also going out.

Sunnyside proved more and more expensive to build, then to maintain. Like Scott, later Mark Twain, and many other writers, Irving was a poor businessman. Most of his investments failed to bring in hoped-for returns, and some of the enterprises into which he put his money failed altogether. He lost on his steamship investment in France. He lost heavily on insurance stock and in real estate speculations. At one point he put $20,000 into lots in Toledo, Ohio. At another time he bought land in Green Bay, Wisconsin, from Astor for $4,000, though this he later sold back to Astor at his purchase price.

Twenty years older than he, Astor was one of his first visitors at Sunnyside. He arrived unexpectedly soon after Irving had moved in in 1836, stayed two days, and left, promising to return when the sleighing was better. Soon, Irving had other guests, and these came to stay.

Ebenezer, ten years his senior, failed in business and came to live in Sunnyside with his daughters. Irving's sister Catherine and her daughter also became part of the family at Sunnyside. Irving was now not only a householder, he was also the responsible head of a numerous family. What he had thought of as a country retreat became their year-round home. A "small mansion" in Irving's stories, Sunnyside was always a "cottage" in his letters. It was a more accurate designation. The house is small. The rooms are small, some of them very small. For the first ten years of his life there, Irving was forced to make his bed on the cot in an alcove of his downstairs study. There were not bedrooms enough for him to have one to himself. The crowded little house with its small rooms, narrow halls and staircases, must sometimes have proved difficult for Irving to work in.

Fortunately he had to be much in New York. His writing and research took him there. His friends were there and his interests were there. America's most famous man of letters, he was loaded down with offices and belabored with offers of more. He was a vice-president of the American Historical Society of Military and Naval Events, a trustee of the New York Society Library, president of the Authors Club. He was kept busy answering requests to speak at dinners, supplying autographs, criticizing the work of hopeful authors, answering letters from people he knew and from many he did not know and had no wish to know.

Always anxious to please, Irving did more than he

wished, but even then was forced to turn down more requests than he could fulfill. He declined to run for Congress during the Jackson administration. He declined to run for mayor of New York on the Tammany Hall ticket.

When his friend Martin Van Buren became President, Irving risked offering advice that would have sounded impertinent from one less intimate with the President-elect, less eminent, or less versed in diplomacy. From New York, February 6, 1837, Irving wrote:

> You have now arrived at the most distinguished post in the world, at the head of the *great republic;* it depends upon yourself to make it the most honorable. There is but one true rule for your conduct; act according to the sound dictates of your head and the kind feelings of your heart, without thinking how temporary popularity is to be affected by it, and *without caring about re election.*

Something of the best of Washington Irving rings in that letter. Something of the shrewd and cautious Irving who knew his own limitations shows in another. Van Buren offered him the Secretaryship of the Navy in his cabinet. In a long reply in which he turned down the offer, Irving said:

> Perhaps, had my ambition led me to a higher career, and aimed at official distinction I might have become enured to the struggle; but it has laid in a different and more secluded path, and has nurtured in me habits of quiet, and a love of peace of mind, that daily unfit me, more and more, from the collisions of the world. I really believe it would take but a

> short career of public life at Washington to render me mentally and physically a perfect wreck, and to hurry me prematurely into old age.

Fifteen years before in "The Author" Geoffrey Crayon had written, "My only aim is to paint characters and manners. I am no politician."

Irving refused public office for himself, but, marking his letter confidential, he wrote to Van Buren in 1838 asking for some kind of government job for Ebenezer. At another time he suggested a nephew, Theodore Irving, for a naval appointment.

After finishing his western books, Irving had begun to gather material for a contemplated book on the Spanish conquest of Mexico. Learning at the library by accident that William Hickling Prescott was considering a book on the same subject, Irving generously relinquished all title to the project, leaving a clear field for the younger man. The act cost Irving more than Prescott knew at the time. He had no other literary project in mind which might produce the immediate income he felt he needed.

Though after his one early experience with the *Analectic* he had consistently refused every offer, even Scott's, of editorship on periodicals, he gladly accepted an offer from the *Knickerbocker Magazine* to write for it regularly at a salary of $2,000 annually. Gratified at having obtained the services of the writer in whose honor his magazine had been named, its editor, Lewis Gaylord Clark, described his new contributor. "A gleam of genuine pleasure laughed in his eye. In dress simple—in manners gentle and easily entreated—he takes the hue of the time and the taste of his company so gracefully upon himself, that you think you have known him for years."

Irving wrote steadily for the *Knickerbocker* for two and a half years, a long stint for a writer generally averse to such labor.

Peter Irving had been abroad for twenty-seven years. After much hesitation—partly because the sickly doctor feared seasickness—he returned to the United States. Irving was delighted to have him with all the rest of them at Sunnyside, but Peter later moved into New York to be nearer the activities in which he was interested.

On March 15, 1838, Judge John Treat Irving died at fifty-eight. On July 27 of the same year, Peter died. His death, coming within a few months of that of their brother, was particularly hard on Washington Irving. "I feel how completely Peter and myself were intertwined together in the whole course of our existence," he wrote Sarah Van Wart. ". . . I have been so accustomed to talk over every plan with him and, as it were, to think aloud when in his presence, that I cannot open a book, or take up a paper, or recall a past vein of thought, without having him instantly before me, and finding myself completely overcome."

It was with Peter that Irving had spent so many of his years abroad in England, France, and Spain. Thoughts of Peter made Irving miss Europe the more. Too politic to express such opinions in public, Irving—like the bitterly outspoken James Fenimore Cooper who expressed them vehemently—was not altogether happy with life in the United States. He loved Sunnyside. He was happy with his family, his friends, and his varied engagement in New York, but he wrote a friend in Paris, "Good Lord deliver me from the all-pervading commonplace which is the curse of our country."

Irving shrank from running for elective office. He many

times refused high government appointments in Washington; but he had never made it a secret among his powerfully placed friends that he could easily be induced to accept the proper diplomatic post. Yet he seems to have been genuinely surprised when the offer came.

Daniel Webster, who as Secretary of State had suggested the appointment to President John Tyler, knew that it had been made—and knew that by the time he spoke Irving would have been notified—when he said, "Washington Irving is now one of the most astonished men in the city of New York." Political enemies joined in applauding this appointment. Henry Clay, long one of Irving's friends, and Senator William C. Preston of South Carolina, who reported favorably for the Senate Committee on Foreign Relations, were as pleased as Webster.

On February 10, 1842, Washington Irving was made Envoy Extraordinary and Minister Plenipotentiary to the Court of Spain.

"Nothing was more unexpected. It was perfectly unsolicited," said Washington Irving, as pleased as he was surprised. He had always loved Spain. He had spent happy and busy years there. He was glad to return. The high office would not only give him financial security, but also leisure to work on his long-contemplated, long-deferred biography of George Washington. Prescott called to meet Irving at about this time. His host was in high spirits. "Found him delightful—and what they say is rare—wide awake."

Irving had one social duty to perform before he could

Sailing from New York, April 1842

leave for his new post. The most famous writer in the United States had to introduce the most famous writer of England at a great banquet in New York. The fastidious Irving was appalled at Dickens whom he thought coarse in manner and vulgar in dress, but none of his distaste showed when he rose to introduce the popular novelist. It was Irving's old inability to speak in public which floored him. He said loudly, "Charles Dickens, guest of the Nation!" and sat down to tremendous applause.

Genuinely attracted to Irving as he had been deeply influenced by his books, Dickens was far more effusive. "Everything you have written is upon my shelves, and in my thoughts, and in my heart of hearts," he told Irving. He said he had worn out his copy of the Knickerbocker history by carrying it in his pocket. In a letter he described himself as "a man who loves you and holds communion with your spirit oftener perhaps than any other person alive."

Irving's New York friends were eager to tender the new minister another testimonial dinner such as they had staged for him just ten years before. Irving was relieved that he could plead as excuse that he was too busy preparing to leave for Spain. On April 10, 1842, Washintgon Irving sailed from New York on the *Independence.*

chapter XIII

Irving loitered in England. As an American of ambassadorial rank as well as a famous author, he was presented to Queen Victoria. He talked with Lord John Russell and with England's Prime Minister, Sir Robert Peel. He spent as much time as he could with old friends like Thomas Moore, and he lived in London where of all places he would have chosen to live.

He stayed with a British Foreign Office friend in the Little Cloisters of Westminster Abbey itself. As, wonderingly, he wrote to a sister in Tarrytown, he actually lived in what had been one of his romantic and meditative haunts while he was writing *The Sketch Book* more than twenty years before. It was like his living in the Alhambra after writing *The Conquest of Granada* and in Sunnyside after writing "The Legend of Sleepy Hollow." "Am I always to have my dreams turned into realities?"

From London, Irving went on to Paris where he visited with his niece, Sarah Storrow. Though it had not for him the charm it had exerted in earlier years—or so he said—he mingled in Paris society. In Paris he was joined by the two principal members of his staff. He had chosen Alexander Hamilton, grandson of the first Secretary of the Treasury, as secretary of the American legation in Spain; and Carson Brevoort, son of his old friend, as attaché.

He had written about the country and its people in a way which made clear his love for both. Irving was well known and greatly admired in Spain. He was warmly welcomed in Madrid. In a deep sense, he was home again, home in spirit. He knew everybody of importance in diplomatic circles, and he was *persona grata* to those about the Spanish court whose opinion mattered most.

One of his first duties was to call with Hamilton—both men in formal diplomatic uniform—and present his credentials to the queen. They found Queen Isabella in the vast, silent, and almost empty palace. Isabella, not yet twelve years of age, received them in company with her younger sister, her governess, and her guardian, Argüelles. All were in deep mourning for the Duke of Orleans. Irving was touched at the sight of the child queen and princess. They were carefully tended and treated with all the deference due to royalty, but they were child pawns to be maneuvered by the real rulers of empire.

The power in Spain when Irving presented his credentials was General Baldomero Espartero. Espartero, Duke of Victoria and Duke of Morella, ruled as regent of the constitutional monarchy. Forceful and stern but frank and open, he was "a soldier of fortune" whom Irving greatly admired.

Espartero had risen to power through the army. He had fought against Napoleon, then for eight years against the revolting Spanish colonists in America. In the struggle for supremacy in Spain, he had defeated the supporters of Don Carlos and become the established leader of the liberal party. He was virtually a dictator in Spain when Irving arrived as minister.

Irving was active and conscientious in his role as minister. He wrote and dispatched long reports to the Secretaries of State—successively Daniel Webster, John C. Calhoun, and James Buchanan. These reports were informed, detailed, and sensible. Coming from Irving, they were clear. Webster always put aside any other work when a dispatch came in from Irving.

The American minister made the continual round of calls expected of him. He attended frequent formal, and often tiring, court ceremonies. He found the duties of office exceeded what he had expected. They left him little free time for writing. What leisure he had he expended as much in long, colorful letters to his family, describing the court and life in Madrid, as on his literary work.

The American legation had for quarters one-half of the spacious hotel of the Duke of San Lorenzo, the other half being occupied by the Brazilian legation. The Americans were well housed and well served. Lorenzo was Irving's valet and personal servant. Juana was housekeeper. Pedro was coachman, and Antonio was cook. There were various underservants, including a footboy to run errands for the minister and his assistants.

Irving described them all in his letters. Usually he rose about five o'clock in the morning to thwart the hot Spanish sun. He read and wrote letters until about eight, when Hamilton and Brevoort joined him at breakfast. As they read their newspapers and letters, they listened to the military band marching through the street below their windows for the changing of the guard at the palace. A little later they could hear another band coming back.

Irving spent most of the day in his huge high-ceilinged bedroom and study, as the others did in theirs. They walked back and forth to discuss various matters or just to gossip. Like all Spanish houses in summer, the hotel of the Duke of San Lorenzo was kept cool by drawn shades and blinds, with just light enough admitted for Irving and his staff to read by. The Americans dined at five o'clock, took their siesta in the Spanish fashion, then, unless some function demanded their presence, strolled on the Prado. Sometimes Irving just spent the cool of the evening on his balcony, watching the lights and the life of the capital.

Every evening the royal coach, drawn by six horses, drove past. In an open barouche, the small queen and her sister were surrounded by a troop of horse. Irving liked to watch the queen returning from her drive. He felt for "these poor innocent little beings in whose isolated state I take a great interest."

In 1843 Irving had far more than his daily routine to report. Espartero's opposition gathered its forces and attacked the capital. The general alarm was sounded.

Newspapers were suspended and shops were closed as the streets of the besieged city filled with armed men. Shots were fired, and it was feared that the palace itself would be attacked. Concerned for the safety of the royal children, Irving suggested that the entire diplomatic corps go to the palace to stand by the queen.

The insurrectionists triumphed. Espartero was deposed and driven into exile in England. The aristocracy swept back into power, and the old nobility took over again. The palace, which had been almost deserted, was now thronged with gaily costumed courtiers, victorious generals, and ambitious statesmen. The young queen, regal amidst the uproar, was legally declared of age. The regency was ended, and haste was being made to find a politically useful royal husband for the child.

With the diplomats from other nations, Irving had to pay his respects to a new set of Spanish officials, the successful counter-plotters now fawning upon the child queen. The queen mother returned from exile in Paris to be reunited with her children in splendid ceremony that took place twenty-seven miles from Madrid. According to Spanish custom, the children went part way to meet her. Though he was already suffering a return of his old malady, an inflammation of the ankles which made it difficult and painful for him to walk or even to stand for any length of time, Irving was present with the other diplomats accredited to Spain.

Fagged by his official and personal correspondence, Irving went to France for his health in the autumn of 1843. His health did not improve. Seemingly the concentration required in study and writing produced the nervous affliction. In January 1844, when he was sixty, Irving wrote, ". . . disheartened by the continuance of my malady, which obliges me to abstain from all literary occupation, and half disables me for social intercourse."

By April he was feeling a little better, well enough to give two diplomatic dinners. Some of his usual good humor and even spirit returned, but he was lonely and felt a little sorry for himself. Alexander Hamilton and Carson Brevoort, on whom he had depended for companionship as well as for official aid, resigned, and he missed them badly. He was depressed, too, by some aspects of the Madrid court. He wrote Sarah Storrow in Paris, "I am wearied and at times heartsick of the wretched politics of this country, where there is so much intrigue, falsehood, profligacy, and crime, and so little of high honor and pure patriotism in political affairs."

He added what is as close to a note of pessimism as Irving ever uttered. "The last ten or twelve years of my life . . . has shown me so much of the dark side of human nature, that I begin to have painful doubts of my fellow men, and look back with regret to the confiding period of my literary career, when, poor as a rat, but rich in dreams, I beheld the world through the medium of my imagination, and was apt to believe men as good as I wish them to be."

Irving exaggerated. He had never been "poor as a rat," not the ordinary rat, anyway; and he had never been that naive.

His spirits improved and so did his health. Jasper Livingston, son of Supreme Court Justice Brockholst Livingston, arrived to become his new legation secretary. Irving took a holiday in Barcelona, in which he delighted. He traveled to Avignon. He went to England and spent three weeks in Birmingham, where he was always happy. In France he called on King Louis Philippe and the royal family at Versailles.

He returned to the full swing of ambassadorial functions and social life in Spain, to the life he enjoyed, but he spent more of his time alone. Writing had got him used to solitude, and he was writing again at his *Washington* and other biographical projects. He knew the uses of solitude for work and even for a kind of pleasure. Looking back, he saw his life ". . . crowded with incidents and personages, and full of shifting scenes and sudden transitions. All these I can summon up and cause to pass before me, and in this way can pass hours together in a kind of reverie."

This was a passing mood in exile in enervating Spain, and part of the lassitude of convalescence. Before long, Irving would be racing with energy and driving at new self-imposed writing tasks. Irving showed more purposeful determination in his later than in his earlier years. His strength was returning in full. On his sixty-second birthday in 1845 he was surprised to find himself running upstairs three steps at a time. He checked himself to a more dignified ambassadorial pace.

In December 1845 Irving resigned his post in Madrid. He went immediately to England. Louis McLane, again minister to England, felt that Irving's presence there would be valuable in a new crisis. England and the United States were in bitter dispute over the northern boundary of Oregon. Irving knew most of the important people in the British government. He was on terms of friendship with them and enjoyed their confidence. These qualifications could be important.

Irving did his best. As part of his effort to help, he wrote an article presenting the American side of the question to the British public. He strongly upheld the United States claim to possession of all of Oregon up to the forty-ninth parallel of latitude. He felt it was important that the country have full control of the Columbia River.

His task in England finished, Irving returned to Paris to say goodbye to his niece, Sarah Storrow, who was about to set off on a visit to the United States. Then, traveling day and night, he went on to Madrid. Completely well again, he was anxious to have done with diplomacy and get back to his writing. He was back in Madrid in March, but he had to curb his impatience. A successor as minister to Spain had not even been appointed.

Not until July did General Romulus M. Saunders of North Carolina reach Madrid as the new minister. Irving then bade official farewell to the young queen. Queen Isabella responded with the correct expressions of national regret but added for herself, "Your distinguished personal merits have gained in my heart the appreciation which you merit by more than one title."

Irving reached London again in mid-August 1846. He delayed only long enough to say a few goodbyes, then boarded a steamship for Boston, where he arrived September 18, 1846. The next day he took a river boat from New York to Tarrytown. He had been away four and a half years. Reinvigorated and determined, he was home at Sunnyside again.

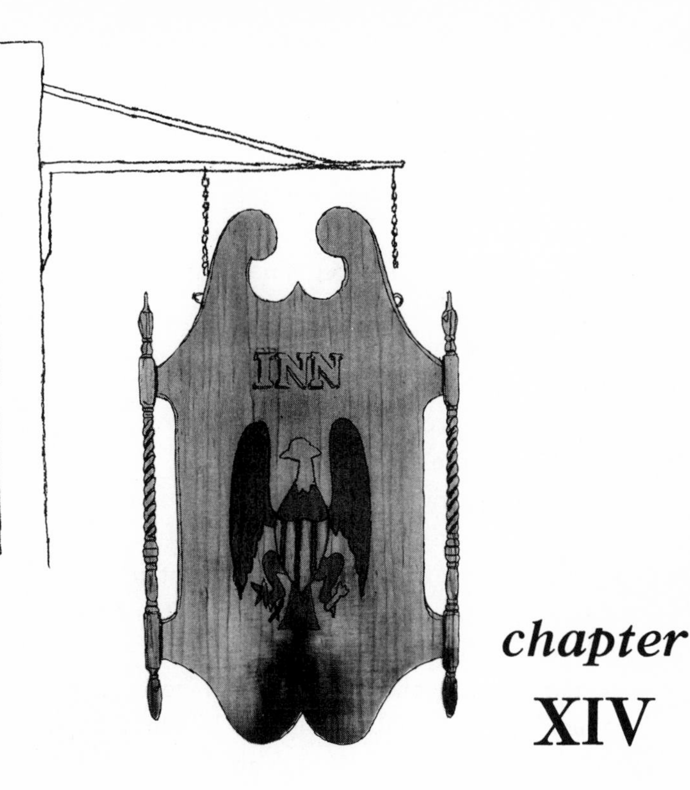

chapter XIV

Washington Irving at sixty-three was hardly the brash young blade who had frolicked in Cockloft Hall and dashed off the certitudes of *Salmagundi*, or the fashionable young gentleman who had sailed on his sentimental pilgrimage to England in 1815. Neither was he the dream-filled romantic who had drunk his fill in the Alhambra. All men, of course, change with the years, but with Irving the change was more marked than that which comes with the mere wear and tear of time and experience.

Irving, as the phrase is, had never settled down. Henry Leavitt Ellsworth, the sharp-eyed Yankee Indian Commissioner with whom Irving had ridden and bivouacked on the prairies, had shrewdly prophesied that Irving would never marry. He enjoyed the society of attractive women, but, as Ellsworth wrote his wife, he was "too much a man of the world to fasten his affections and confine his favors." Ellsworth, who liked and admired his famous companion, reported, too, that Irving lived and wrote on the surface of life.

Irving had never married, and he had consistently refused all of the government sinecures offered him again and again. His diplomatic posts had come as formal recognition of his literary success, and were of a different order. He had shrunk from business and from practice of the law. He had never been a participant in the life of the country or in the ordinary workaday life of the world. He had remained an observer, not an analytical but a curious and tolerant observer who did not take sides.

Life had been a spectator sport for Washington Irving. He sat in the stands or strolled about the edge of the crowd. Despite his interest in the game and in the scene, he remained detached in smiling aloofness. Just as he preferred not to become embroiled in political dispute, he avoided emotional entanglements which might disturb the serenity he liked best. Cautiously he lived a long-protracted youth.

Instinctively, Irving avoided anything which might jar his serenity or impede the free and even flow of the thoughts and feelings he carefully transferred to paper. Fastidious about his person, he was always clean-shaven, scrubbed, and in fresh linen when he sat down to write. It was as if he had to wash away the grubbiness of the real world before he could achieve the detachment that marks his work. He protected the temperament that gives his writing its cheerful and equable tone.

Now, Washington Irving, who had so long eschewed domestic responsibility and strong emotional ties, undertook those of home and family. His brothers had worked for him. He worked now for Peter and Ebenezer and his daughters. The carefree traveler became the fixed householder and the paterfamilias. Perhaps because he was a little tired and lonely, he took on gladly the emotional and economic obligations he had long studiously avoided.

Irving changed. He could change in this way because there was one constant and unchanging element in him, his talent as a writer.

Here there is a remarkable consistency about Washington Irving. His talent was the direct expression of his character, and in character and its expression he seems to have been all of one piece from the beginning. He began with a developed skill, manifest in *Salmagundi.* The flippancy of youth became a quieter humor, but he used the same style, the same approach, the same manner, in *The Sketch Book* and in *Bracebridge Hall.* These qualities stay unchanged, despite weightier subjects, in his later books.

Irving was more sensitive than most. He was more imaginative. He preferred the misted past to the glare of the present, but in many ways he was comfortingly like everybody else. He enjoyed his childhood with his brothers and sisters. He was bored at school, happier out of doors. As a young man he derided what he disliked or what he did not understand. He felt the same emotions, the same sentiments, that most people feel.

Irving liked people about him, the best people. He liked pretty women. He smoked. He sometimes drank too much wine. Probably he ate too much, for it was the custom of the time. He disliked regular work and, unless fascinated by some compelling subject, avoided it. He preferred play. Even more, he preferred doing nothing. Indolence and lassitude are only literary terms for what the Victorians condemned as laziness and modern American civilization applauds as leisure. Most people have always liked it, and they liked seeing Irving celebrate and practice it in *The Sketch Book* and his other books of essays and stories.

Irving was often depressed, more often in his earlier years as a writer from doing nothing than from trying to do too much. When he was really interested, he worked tirelessly and, though sometimes disappointed in his daily performance, without depression. He felt or affected a distaste for politics, but he liked intelligent politicians. He liked especially the rewards of office and, when he could, enjoyed the advantages and perquisites of appointive diplomatic posts. Irving associated with the people who could and did advance his career. When he had a surfeit of all he wanted, he went to sleep, whether at dinner or on a social call. Irving was very human. There is just one principal difference. He could write as no American had written before him and as few have written since.

Irving had not the stubbornness of James Fenimore Cooper who, as Mark Twain pointed out, made an almost unbelievable number of literary errors on every page. He had not the qualities of some of the great writers, who followed him. He had not Twain's western tang and American *sang-froid*. He had not Emerson's brilliant insight or eloquence. He lacked Poe's cleverness and ingenuity. There is not the thought in Irving that there is in Hawthorne, or the occasional sublimity. He did not have Longfellow's touch for the popular taste in fluent verse.

This is only another way of saying that Irving had other qualities of his own. Those who followed him had him for model. Longfellow, Hawthorne, and Lowell were outspoken in their praise and in acknowledging their debt to him.

When Irving wrote, there was no substantial body of American writing and no body of American writers. Like other people of his time who read at all, he read the classic English writers. Irving was imbued with their spirit and their style before he was a writer at all. He soaked up their manner and their methods through his pores when he was a boy. It was Addison, Steele, Goldsmith his friends knew, read, and imitated. It was English writers and writings they discussed at their "bibulous and carnivorous" gatherings.

Irving was almost in himself a transition and a translation. He was a transition from the Old World to the New. He was a transition from the colonial and Federal world to the democratic world of Andrew Jackson which, at first, at any rate, he disliked. He was transition from literary dependence upon England to some literary independence in the United States. He translated English traditions to Americans, who were still largely people of British descent. He translated America and American themes to the British.

Both countries were bitter after the War of 1812. The United States resented the wanton destruction of Washington during that war and feared other depredations. England sneered at uncouth Americans. Washington Irving, absorbing what was best in the British spirit, painted the ancestral country in kinder terms for his American readers. At the same time he showed England that the United States was not just an untamed wilderness inhabited by white as well as red savages.

Some writers are intensely concerned with the movements and problems of their time. They feel strongly and sometimes write blazingly about contemporary issues. Others writers, instinctively or through temperament, avoid such subjects. They hark back to the simple and unchanging. They stay with the elemental facts of life and death, the passage of time, the notions and emotions of men and women. They do not take sides and make decisions on transient ideas and events.

They watch the broad stream of life, not the swirls and eddies which disturb it. They live with what seems to them of lasting significance. They may do this well or they may do it badly. Washington Irving was one of those who did it well. In turning down proffered government appointments he said, as he said several times to various people on other occasions, that he felt he was of greater value portraying the American people for all to see than taking part in partisan issues.

Washington Irving did one thing that the writer whose work is to last must do. He gave pleasure. He gave pleasure to the people of his time, and he has given pleasure to generations of readers since.

What kind of pleasure? Charm, gentle humor, pleasant scenes, quiet reflection, likeable characters. In most people there is a degree of liking for what is old and has become quaint. Today's farmer with tractors the size of battleships in his yard will still have old dobbin's halter tacked to the wall in his barn. Whether they live in Brown County, Indiana, in the mountains of northern Georgia, or in England's Devon, people know the Sleepy Hollow of a century and a half ago because Irving showed them one in Westchester County, New York.

The man or woman listening to an organ in a city church —or in a country church, for that matter—can feel something of what Irving felt in Westminster Abbey. People celebrating Christmas enjoy it the more for knowing how the Squire and Master Simon enjoyed the season in Bracebridge Hall. The man in love, or the woman, can recognize some of his own feelings in *The Sketch Book*. Those who have known grief feel it shared.

You need not have ridden in a stagecoach to know the joys of travel through the English countryside. If you have ridden a horse or in a wagon or on a bicycle or even in a car, you share some of what Washington Irving experienced, and let you experience, in his travels a long time ago. You need not have been in Abbotsford or in Dresden or in the Alhambra to know what he felt on his journeys to strange and colorful places in the 1820s and the 1840s. You recognize what he felt when you go to New York or the Grand Canyon or wherever.

You don't have to gallop along in a swaying chaise or clip-clop behind Dolly or Dandy or bump over the waves for a month in a sailing ship. Any wheel is a good wheel that takes you from the overly familiar to the wonderfully strange, from monotony to variety, and a jet engine or two or four can do as well as a mainsail. You like motion. Irving liked motion. It's a shared thing and a kinship. Thank you, Mr. Irving.

The way he wrote about places and people, buffalo or ghosts, accounts for much of the charm that Irving exerts. He wrote musically, melodiously. There is no sharpness, no harshness. Nothing jars. He had the clarity of eighteenth-century prose in his nineteenth-century tales and sketches. There is the sunniness of Sunnyside and his own temperament in some of it; the shadows of the glens and brooks of Sleepy Hollow in some of it; the music of his flute on occasion; and sometimes the pleasantly muted music of sadness without pain in it.

That is the way Irving wrote because he was Irving. It is also the way he wrote because that was the style he valued. He valued style above content, for he felt that style lasted after content was gone. If he read only for meaning, a man might read once, then promptly forget. If the style soothed, pleased, enchanted, he would read again for pleasure in the music, the color, the rhythms, the glow of words and sentences.

Irving's writing is light, as his nature was light. He lived and wrote near the surface. This lack of depth is not bad any more than profundity is necessarily good. Irving disliked extremes. Neither ecstacy nor black tragedy were to his taste. He preferred the placid, the mildly comic, the reverie in the churchyard. He liked violence only when it was sugar-coated by chivalry. The reader can go elsewhere for his thrills.

Irving liked children. Their innocence appealed to him. He romped with them. With their elders he could be deftly polite and practically expedient when he had to be. Diplomacy went well with his genial humor. Though he cared little about causes, he had ideals of generosity and decent conduct between men and between nations. He avoided taking sides in most disputes because even minor conflict disturbed him. He wanted to be liked, and stern men of stern principles inevitably make stern enemies.

Irving winced under attack and sometimes nearly collapsed under even rumored displeasure with him or any of his books. The man of the world and famous writer always needed reassurance from brothers, from friends like Brevoort, and later from his nieces. With all the real modesty that was his, the dependence such need betrays has its own appeal. The reader sometimes feels protective toward Irving and enjoys indulgence of the feeling.

Irving was nostalgic, wistful for what he thought of as good in an older day, just as we can sometimes feel wistful for some of the elegance of his. Irving wrote sketches, not sharply plotted tales or melodramatic scenes. He wrote of battles, sometimes of murder, but the tales were old. The violence had faded out of them. They were just tales.

Irving's genius was not marked by eccentricity. It was marked by decency, small faults, great care for his art. He was shy when called upon to speak in public, but he liked to parade in costume in amateur theatricals when he was among appreciative friends. Modesty, kindliness, and humor are attractive qualities in a great man. Irving had them.

A woman who met him at about the time of his return from Spain in 1846 described him in these words: ". . . man of about sixty, with large, beautiful eyes, a large, well-formed nose, a countenance still handsome . . . youthfully fresh and humorous disposition and soul." She noted that his face was unlined and that he had no gray hair. He had none that showed. As people close to him knew, Irving wore a dark wig.

Some time earlier the brilliant English actress Fanny Kemble, who spent a dozen years in this country, had thrown her arms about Irving when she met him, exclaiming that he seemed so English he reminded her of home. She thought him "modestly superior to his countrymen." (Perhaps by way of returning the compliment, Irving's nieces, who were ecstatic about Miss Kemble and her acting, named their pet pig at Sunnyside "Fanny Kemble.")

James Russell Lowell dispatched other writers concisely, and sometimes with derision, in his "Fable for Critics." When he came to characterize Washington Irving his tone changed. He was faced with a problem: how fix Irving's identity? He solved his problem perhaps in the only way he could, but nicely.

But allow me to speak what I honestly feel,—
To a true poet-heart add the fun of Dick Steele,
Throw in all of Addison, *minus* the chill,
With the whole of that partnership's stock and good-will,
Mix well, and while stirring, hum o'er, as a spell,
The fine *old* English gentleman, simmer it well,
Sweeten just to your own private liking, then strain,
That only the finest and purest remain,
Let it stand out of doors till a soul it receives
From the warm lazy sun loitering down through green leaves,
And you'll find a choice nature, not wholly deserving
A name either English or Yankee,—just Irving.

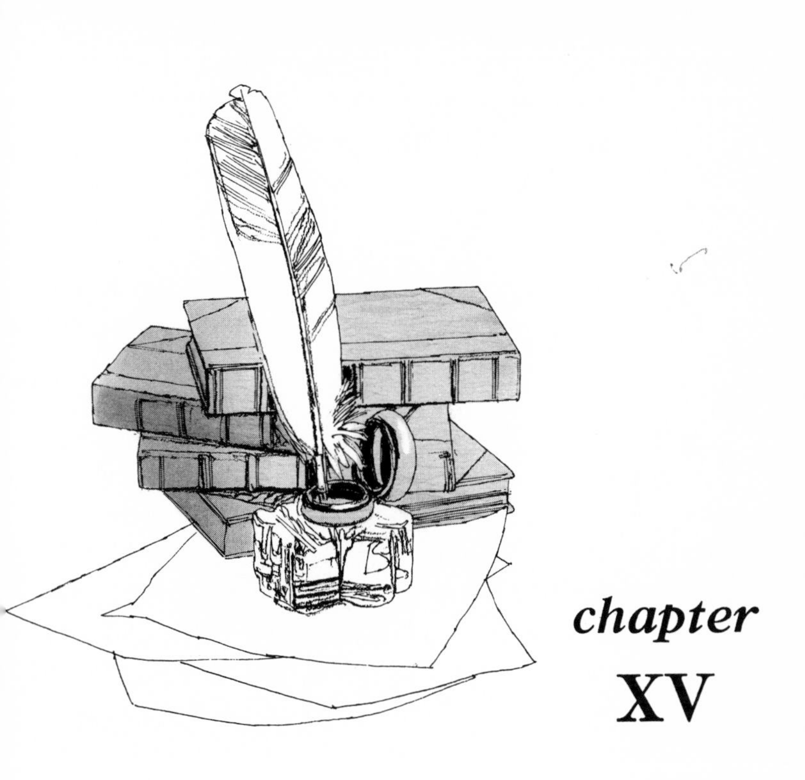

chapter XV

Washington Irving was one of the country's most honored, even beloved, figures when he returned to Sunnyside in 1846. Undoubtedly he knew it, and undoubtedly he was pleased, but he was far too intent on other matters to spend much time basking in his popularity or being awed by his stature.

He was amazed at the changes in his native New York, now a city of over 370,000. "New York as you knew it," he wrote his sister in Birmingham, who had not been home in forty years, "was a mere corner of the present city; and that corner is all changed, pulled to pieces, burnt down, and rebuilt. . . . It is really now one of the most racketing cities in the world and reminds me of one of the great European cities (Frankfort for instance) in the time of an annual fair. Here it is a fair almost all the year round."

Irving was in the city often, but his life centered in Sunnyside. Brother and nieces had been there to welcome its master home when he returned from Spain. His study awaited him. His gardens, horses, cows, and dogs were all in fine condition. The household was as glad to welcome him home as he was to be there.

Immediately Irving set about building an addition. It really was a new building, a tall pagoda-like tower connected by a passage to the peak-gabled house. He had the kitchen and stable yard enclosed to make a large farmyard for his poultry. He dug a new ice pond and built a new ice house. He had trees cut and pruned to afford a better view of the river. He loved to look from the windows of his dining room and drawing room out over the wide Tappan Zee where there were usually ships passing and sloops at anchor.

With ambitious literary plans formed, Irving was getting his whole house in order. On his return to the United States he found to his dismay that his Philadelphia publishers, protesting that there was no longer a ready market for them, had allowed many of his early books to go out of print and did not intend to issue new editions. Irving was hurt and disturbed. He was spending heavily on Sunnyside, and the lack of income from his books could be serious. His investments in western lands had not begun to pay appreciable dividends, and most of his other investments provided none. As his books were being pirated in England—reprinted without payment to the author—that income, too, had fallen away.

In New York he was using a desk in the law office of his nephew John Irving. Jokingly, Irving said he might have to return to the practice of law to earn a living.

At about this juncture George Palmer Putnam returned from eight years in London where he had been associated with John Murray. He knew the commercial as well as the literary value of Irving's books. He approached Irving with an offer to issue a collected edition of all of his books, each revised by the author, to be published in uniform volumes. He offered Irving $2,000 a year and guaranteed an increasing sum each year from royalties to be paid on all copies sold. Irving gladly accepted.

He went to work quickly on the revisions, and as quickly Putnam's issued them. The books were very successful. Critics vied with each other in praising books which had already become classics. Younger readers, to whom many of them were new, accepted them enthusiastically. Irving lost no time. In and out of New York to dine with Astor or other friends, to work in the library, to go to the theater, he was at work on his *Alhambra*.

A catastrophe threatened at Sunnyside. Irving, almost as much the country gentleman now as Squire Bracebridge, was aghast when the long-talked-of plan to build a railroad from New York to Albany along the eastern shore of the Hudson was put into operation. As Sunnyside was atop a wooded bank almost at the river's edge, he feared the trains would either run through his study or so close to the house as to make it uninhabitable. He declared indignantly that if the Garden of Eden were on earth, men would not hesitate to run a railroad through it.

Protest was useless so, as usual, Irving made the best of it. The tracks were actually laid on filled land in the

water, so they did not run through the house, but they were—and still are—so close that the hooting and tooting of the trains disturbed all the family. With the building of the new addition, Irving had finally achieved the luxury of a bedroom of his own. Unable to sleep for the noise of the trains beneath its windows, Irving gave up this room on the river side of Sunnyside and moved across the hall where the noise was not quite so loud.

The only redeeming feature of the change was that the railroad company paid Irving $3,500 as damages for land taken. He said it was the only real estate transaction on which he had ever made money.

For part of 1848 he was at John Jacob Astor's working on his life of George Washington. Astor died, and Irving, as one of his executors, spent most of a year in New York helping to settle the estate. Long before, he had suggested to Astor that he found a library. Astor had not done so at the time but left provisions in his will for the establishment of the Astor Library. Irving helped set it up and became its first president. The Astor Library was joined later with the Tilden and Lenox to become the great New York Public Library at Forty-second Street and Fifth Avenue. Irving can thus be looked upon as one of its founders.

In 1849 Irving published his biography of Oliver Goldsmith. This was expanded from a slight sketch written years before to introduce a selection of Goldsmith's writing. Irving apologized for the inadequacy of his treatment, explaining that he had been forced to write it hurriedly while under pressure from other demands on his time and attention. Yet the book was a tribute he wished to pay. Goldsmith's writings, he said, "were the delight of my childhood, and have been a source of enjoyment to me throughout life."

In 1849 and 1850 Irving published his two-volume *Mahomet and His Successors.* This was a delayed by-product of his work in Spanish history. Years before he had planned a sketch of the founder of Islam in order to explain more fully the Moorish conquest of Spain. The work had been pushed aside until he could revise it during the latter part of his ministry in Madrid.

Five years later, in 1855, Irving issued a collection of stray stories and essays, some of which had first appeared in the *Knickerbocker,* under the title of *Wolfert's Roost.* Diedrich Knickerbocker himself, so Irving said, had once stayed in what was now his home. The title story is of the house that became Sunnyside and of its eccentric inhabitants, but others in the collection are legends of old Spain, and one substantial piece is a history of the financial legerdemain of John Law and "The Great Mississippi Bubble."

All of these books added to the sum of Irving's literary accomplishment, but one other was foremost in his mind, his *Life of George Washington.* This was to be the crowning achievement of his career. He had planned it many years before. He had gathered material for it in England, in libraries, from anecdotes, from the public archives of the United States. Often he had started to write it; as often, other work or illness had interfered. Long since the hard-working professional of firmly established repute, Irving was intent on ending his career with what he felt sure would be a lasting work. He was not writing for reputation now. He had all any man could use. He was not writing for money, though he could always use more of that. He was working to know full expression of his powers, to realize himself completely through major creation. A compulsion drove him. He seemed to feel that writing this book was a debt he owed George Washington, the world, and himself.

Irving was recognized now as the reigning monarch of American letters. Friends, strangers, other writers paid court to him by letter or by calls at Sunnyside. He was the undisputed king of American literature, but he was a modest monarch whether at home in what he always called his "den" or hurrying down Broadway with his wig firm on his head but his cloak flying about him.

The even more modest Nathaniel Hawthorne sent him a copy of his newly-published *Blithedale Romance.* He wrote that he had wanted to introduce himself ever since he began to write, but that he had hesitated to send any of his earlier books. Sending *Blithedale,* Hawthorne said, "affords me—and I ask no more—an opportunity of expressing the affectionate admiration which I have felt so long; a feeling, by the way, common to all our countrymen in reference to Washington Irving . . ."

Something of a king himself in the literary court of Boston and Cambridge, Dr. Oliver Wendell Holmes called at Sunnyside to pay his respects to one whom "The Autocrat of the Breakfast Table" really respected.

Strangers wrote and, though he complained of the burdensome task, Irving answered all their letters. Autograph seekers found their way to rural Sunnyside, interrupting Irving even when he was at work in his book-lined study. His devoted nieces tried to protect him. Pierre Munro Irving, who had first helped him with the Astor papers, was a New York lawyer. He relinquished most of his other interests to become his uncle's agent and assistant. He aided in research, checked manuscripts and proofs, became Washington Irving's frequent companion and later his very capable biographer.

Sunnyside was home. New York was his work place, but Irving could never break his habits of travel. He made a trip to Washington in 1853, staying with his friend John P. Kennedy, who was Secretary of the Navy. With President Fillmore's family he made a trip to Mount Vernon, home of his lifelong hero and now his devouring subject. At a White House reception he was mobbed by people wishing to shake hands with the country's most famous author. He delved into the archives of the State Department seeking new material on George Washington. With President Fillmore and President-elect Franklin Pierce and all the cabinet he went to inspect a new naval vessel. He was pleased when Pierce told him that when in office he intended to take care of his Bowdoin classmate and friend Nathaniel Hawthorne. Pierce did when he appointed Hawthorne consul at Liverpool.

Irving made return excursions to Washington. On one of them he boarded the ferry from New York to New Jersey where he would entrain and on it met William Makepeace Thackeray, then on a visit to the United States, and the two men who had already met had a pleasant chat. Irving reached Baltimore after dark that night and stayed at the home of Kennedy's father-in-law, where he was provided with every comfort. The Kennedys were now among his closest friends. Their portraits in oil hung on the river wall of his dining room at Sunnyside.

Irving made excursions up the Hudson. He went to North Carolina with Pierre. He attended a wedding in the Shenandoah Valley. He moved about as freely as ever, but he was getting tired. The long and detailed *Life of George Washington* was taking a heavy toll. He was seventy when he wrote a niece of the Kennedys':

> In sober sadness, I believe it is high time I should throw by the pen altogether; but writing has become a kind of habitude with me, and, unless I have some task on hand to occupy a great part of my time, I am at a loss what to do. After being accustomed to literary research, mere desultory reading ceases to be an occupation. There is as much difference between them, in point of interest, as between taking an airing on horseback and galloping after the hounds. It is pretty hard for an old huntsman to give up the chase.

In 1852 Irving wrote Putnam a letter of thanks and appreciation for the arrangement that was working to their mutual profit. Five years later he did more. Business conditions were bad in 1857. Putnam's, which had suffered additional loss through the mismanagement of a partner, was failing. Other publishers quickly approached Irving with attractive offers. Instead of closing with any of them, Irving bought back the plates of his books which Putnam had been forced to let go, and held them until his publisher could get back on his feet again. He then gave him back his plates and contracts. Others followed Irving's example, and the publishing house was saved.

Volumes one and two of Washington Irving's *Life of George Washington* were published in 1855. Volume three appeared in 1856 and volume four in 1857. It was after the publication of the second volume that William Hickling Prescott wrote Irving, "You have done with Washington just as I thought you would, and, instead of a cold, marble statue of a demi-god, you have made him a being of flesh and blood, like ourselves—one with whom we can have sympathy. The general sentiment of the country has been too decidedly expressed for you to doubt for a moment that this is the portrait of him which is to hold a permanent place in the national gallery."

Prescott had tried in small measure to repay some of the debt he owed Irving for relinquishing the conquest of Mexico to him as a subject by obtaining anecdotes about Washington for him. Prescott's father, who had first been offered the job, had been a Harvard classmate of Washington's secretary, Tobias Lear.

Another historian, George Bancroft, sent Irving his congratulations on *Washington.* John Lothrop Motley, whose *Rise of the Dutch Republic* had just been published, wrote what Irving would have been glad to hear during his painful fears on this very subject in Paris a quarter-century earlier: "It is your good fortune to command not only the respect and admiration of your innumerable readers, but their affection also."

The praise must have been sweet to Irving, but he was feeling harried. He had still to finish the fifth and final volume of his *Washington.* He had his materials, but arrangement of them and construction of the book seemed almost beyond his failing strength. Often enough he had said that he must spin his web and then die, but the web was not done. There were times when he felt it might never be.

He had driven himself too hard, but he had to drive himself still harder. He could not sleep at night. He was suffering from asthma. He felt a little better at the family party on his seventy-fifth birthday, April 3, 1858. "I do not fear death," he said that year, "but I would like to go down with all sails set."

He developed catarrh and was bothered by shortness of breath, but he was in and out of New York to the library and the theater, cheerful and humorous in talk. Pierre Irving was reading and checking the chapters of volume five as Irving wrote them. Irving moved into the city that winter and was forced to consult doctors several times about his nervousness and growing ills. Pierre and his wife went with him when he returned to Sunnyside and stayed there to be near him.

Pierre was able to deliver the first three chapters to the publisher in January 1859. He brought the proofs when they were ready for Irving to see. He carted back novels for Irving to read and sometimes read to him to soothe him at night, when he was most nervous. Pierre took to sleeping in a small hall bedroom, hardly larger than a closet, next to his uncle's room, lest Irving be unwell during the night.

On March 15, 1859, Irving finished the last volume of his *Washington*, handed the pages to Pierre, and sank down exhausted on the red sofa in his study. The final chapters were quickly set in type, and the book was ready by Irving's seventy-sixth birthday on April 3. In a brief preface Irving explained that he had resolved to begin work on his *Washington* thirty years before. He thanked Pierre Munro Irving for his work in revising the manuscript of the final volume and seeing it through the press as a "nervous indisposition" brought on by too close an application to the work had rendered him unfit to do it himself. The book, he said, was "the last labor of his pen."

Gently and quietly Washington Irving took leave of his readers.

> Grateful . . . for the kindly disposition which has greeted each successive volume, and with a profound sense of the indulgence he has experienced from the public through a long literary career, now extending through more than half a century, he resigns his last volume to its fate, with a feeling of satisfaction that he has at length reach the close of his task, and with the comforting assurance that it has been with him a labor of love, and as such has to a certain degree carried with it its own reward.

Irving could rest. He had paid his debt. He had started life with George Washington's blessing. He closed his writing life with his *Life of George Washington*. Soon, he felt, his own life might be written. Overcome by a spasm of coughing, he had to retreat from the family party on his seventy-sixth birthday. He turned over all his diaries, notebooks, and records to Pierre, saying, "Somebody will be writing my life when I am gone, and I wish you to do it." He got back the letters he had written Henry Brevoort and told Pierre where to get those he had written to other people.

Ebenezer was still alive, but he was old. The nieces

watched anxiously over their uncle who was so famous and so tired that he could not sleep. The doctor visited his patient almost every day now and sometimes stayed overnight. Pierre kept a daily, almost an hourly, journal of Irving's days and restless nights. He could document the biography he would write not only from books and papers, but also from daily intercourse with its subject.

Irving had given up riding when he was seventy-two. Gentleman Dick had fallen and tossed him into a laurel bush. Protesting that he was the only one who really understood his saddle horse, he had sold him at the insistence of his family. He no longer rode, but he went out every morning for a drive in his carriage.

He read avidly, devouring the books Pierre supplied. He was particularly happy with a book that revived his memories of Spain. Though he was racked by asthma, he talked with wit and animation to his family and to the visitors who came constantly to ivy-shrouded Sunnyside. Irving was never, in any but the physical sense, an old man. He was as alert as ever, as courteous as ever. He visited nearby friends. He went into New York occasionally. He played whist in the evenings. He attended vestry meetings of Christ Church in Tarrytown. He was both vestryman and warden of the church.

An artist who called upon him on an Indian summer day of 1859 found him in his study. From one window he could look far down the Hudson; from the other across his lawns to the carriage drive from the lane which led down from the Albany Post Road. The artist noted the writing table with its many small drawers, the big easy chair, the bronze candelabra. There was a bright coal fire in the open grate under the dark variegated-marble mantel. Three small pictures brightened the wall. One was of a literary party at Sir Joshua Reynolds'. The other two were pen-and-ink sketches with a little color illustrating scenes from the Knickerbocker history. Irving had picked them up in London many years before.

The guest noted happily that Irving's "mental energy seemed unimpaired" and wrote later, "his genial good-humor was continually apparent." He took part of dinner with his host, then rose to catch his train at the little station a quarter-mile below Sunnyside. Irving followed him into the drawing room and at the door took his hand in both of his and wished him well in all his undertakings.

Nathaniel Parker Willis called. The poet-journalist found Irving somewhat thinner, "but the genial expression of his countenance is unchanged, and his eye as kindly and bright. As to sprightliness of attention and reply, I could see little difference from the Washington Irving of other days. The reports of his illness must have been exaggerated, I thought."

Irving admitted to Willis that time hung heavy on his hands since he had given up writing. He said something which revealed much about him as a writer to another visitor.

One of the editors of the New York *Independent* spent a half-hour with him November 7. He asked which of his books Irving looked back upon with the greatest pleasure. Irving answered that he looked back with satisfaction on no one of them. He wished he had another twenty years of life so that he could rewrite them one by one.

On Monday, November 27, Irving walked about the

grounds of Sunnyside in the morning. The effort tired him, and he breathed with difficulty. At dinner that night he exclaimed over the beauty of a sunset whose light filled the dining room. When he started up to bed at about half-past ten o'clock, his niece Sarah went with him to see that everything was in order and that his medicines were at hand.

Irving gasped, "When will this end?"—the niece thought later that was what he had exclaimed—pressed his hand to his side, clutched at the foot of the bed for support, and fell dead to the floor.

Some years before, when the widening of Beekman Street in New York and the consequent breaking up of the graves and vaults of the Brick Church had necessitated their removal, Irving had had the remains of members of his family reinterred in Tarrytown's Sleepy Hollow Cemetery. He had those of the old Scottish nurse who had held him up for George Washington to bless buried with his mother's and reserved a place next to them for himself.

The flags of New York were lowered to half-mast on news of the death of Washington Irving. On the day of his funeral the city's courts were closed. Tarrytown's stores were shut, and the railroad station, hotel, and public buildings were draped in black that day. So was the statue of Major John André past which the long procession moved. There was a great crowd at Christ Church, where the services were held, and the fields about the graveside were filled with carriages.

Washington Irving, son of William and Sarah S. Irving, was seventy-six years, seven months, and twenty-five days old when he died November 28, 1859. That is all it says on the simple marker on his grave in Sleepy Hollow. His books say all the rest.

Perhaps the ending of one of his many letters to Henry Brevoort says a little of it too. "Give my love to all who love me and remember me kindly to all the rest."

WASHINGTON IRVING

1783 — Born April 3 in New York.
1798 — Began study of law.
1802 — *Letters of Jonathan Oldstyle, Gent.*
1803 — Traveled with Hoffmans to Montreal.
1804–1806 — Traveled in Europe.
1807–1808 — *Salmagundi* with William Irving and James Kirke Paulding.
1809 — Matilda Hoffman died.
A History of New York by Diedrich Knickerbocker
1813–1814 — Edited *Analectic Magazine.*
1814 — Served as military aide of New York governor with rank of colonel.
1815 — Sailed for England.
1819–1820 — *The Sketch Book*
1822 — *Bracebridge Hall*
1822–1823 — Spent winter in Dresden.
1824 — *Tales of a Traveller*
1826–1829 — Lived in Spain as attaché to American legation in Madrid.
1828 — *The Life and Voyages of Christopher Columbus*

1829 — *A Chronicle of the Conquest of Granada*

1829–1831 — Served as secretary of American legation in London.

1832 — *The Alhambra*

Returned to the United States.

1835 — *A Tour on the Prairies*

Bought Sunnyside.

1836 — *Astoria*

1837 — *The Adventures of Captain Bonneville, U.S.A.*

1842–1846 — Served as American minister to Spain.

1849 — *Life of Oliver Goldsmith*

1849–1850 — *Mahomet and His Successors*

1855 — *Wolfert's Roost*

1855–1859 — *Life of George Washington*

1859 — Died at Sunnyside, November 28.

BIBLIOGRAPHY

Bowers, Claude G. *The Spanish Adventures of Washington Irving*. Boston: Houghton Mifflin Company, 1940.

Brooks, Van Wyck. *The World of Washington Irving*. New York: E. P. Dutton & Co., Inc., 1944.

Duyckinck, Evert A. and George. *Cyclopedia of American Literature*. New York: Charles Scribner, 1866.

Gilder, Rodman. *The Battery*. Boston: Houghton Mifflin Company, 1936.

Hellman, George S. *Washington Irving, Esquire*. New York: Alfred A. Knopf, Inc., 1925.

———, ed. *Letters of Washington Irving to Henry Brevoort*. New York: G. P. Putnam's Sons, 1915.

Irving, Pierre Munro. *The Life and Letters of Washington Irving*. 4 vols. New York: G. P. Putnam's Sons, 1862–1864.

Irving, Washington. *The Works of Washington Irving*. The Kinderhook Edition of Author's Revised Edition. 10 vols. New York: G. P. Putnam's Sons, 1868.

Latrobe, Charles Joseph. *The Rambler in North America, MDCCCXXXII–MDCCCXXXIII*. 2 vols. New York: Harper & Brothers, 1835.

Lossing, Benson. *The Hudson.* Troy, New York: H. B. Nims & Co., 1866.

Penney, Clara Louise, ed. *Washington Irving Diary; Spain 1828–1829.* New York: Hispanic Society of America, 1926.

Putnam, Major George Haven. "Irving," *The Cambridge History of American Literature.* New York: The Macmillan Company, 1917.

Trent, William P. and George S. Hellman, eds. *The Journals of Washington Irving from July 1815 to July 1842.* 3 vols. Boston: The Bibliophile Society, 1919.

Warner, Charles Dudley. *Washington Irving.* Boston: Houghton Mifflin Company, 1882.

Williams, Stanley T. *The Life of Washington Irving.* 2 vols. New York: Oxford University Press, 1935.

———, ed. *Notes While Preparing Sketch Book, &c 1817* (by Washington Irving). New Haven: Yale University Press, 1927.